Creating Meaningful Inquiry in Inclusive Classrooms

In recent years, the concept of teachers as researchers in both special and mainstream school settings has become part of our everyday language. Whilst many educational practitioners will see the need for research within their setting, many may not be familiar with the technical elements they believe are required.

Creating Meaningful Inquiry in Inclusive Classrooms shows how practitioners can engage in a wide range of educational research and explores its value to the practice of teaching and learning. It introduces the Accessible Research Cycle (ARC), an understandable and meaningful framework for classroom and school-based inquiry for educators. This supports practitioner inquiry and validates the role of the practitioner as both practitioner and researcher. The book offers guidance to practitioners on how to use the ARC using familiar language with accompanying illustrative examples from inquiry carried out in special educational settings. It promotes meaningful participation within the inquiry process for all students.

As the learner population in all schools is changing and becoming more complex, the role of practitioners in exploring evidence-based educational solutions to meet the educational entitlement of children is essential. In supporting a research-informed profession within education, this book will empower practitioners to become the agents of change, help them to become reflective, strategic, investigative and inquiring practitioners.

Phyllis Jones is Associate Professor in the Department of Special Education at the University of South Florida, USA.

Teresa Whitehurst is an Independent Research Consultant who works with organisations and charities supporting children with disability.

Jo Egerton is a Research Project Co-ordinator for the Schools Network and the lead Research Coach for their Research Charter Mark Award.

Creating Meaningful Inquiry in Inclusive Classrooms

Practitioners' stories of research

Edited by Phyllis Jones, Teresa Whitehurst and Jo Egerton

Routledge
Taylor & Francis Group

LONDON AND NEW YORK

First published 2012
by Routledge
2 Park Square, Milton Park, Abingdon, Oxon OX14 4RN

Simultaneously published in the USA and Canada
by Routledge
711 Third Avenue, New York, NY 10017

Routledge is an imprint of the Taylor & Francis Group, an informa business

British Library Cataloguing in Publication Data
A catalogue record for this book is available from the British Library

Library of Congress Cataloging in Publication Data
Creating meaningful inquiry in inclusive classrooms: practitioners' stories of research/edited by Phyllis Jones, Teresa Whitehurst and Jo Egerton.
 p. cm.
Includes bibliographical references and index.
ISBN 978-0-415-67616-8 (hardback) — ISBN 978-0-415-67617-5 (paperback) — ISBN 978-0-203-11267-0 (ebook) 1. Inclusive education. 2. Inclusive education—Research. 3. Education—Research. I. Jones, Phyllis. II. Whitehurst, Teresa. III. Egerton, Jo.
LC1201.C74 2012
371.9'046—dc23   2011052095

ISBN: 978-0-415-67616-8 (hbk)
ISBN: 978-0-415-67617-5 (pbk)
ISBN: 978-0-203-11267-0 (ebk)

Typeset in Galliard
by RefineCatch Limited, Bungay, Suffolk, UK

MIX
Paper from
responsible sources
FSC
www.fsc.org   FSC® C004839

Printed and bound in Great Britain by
TJ International Ltd, Padstow, Cornwall

I am not a social scientist interested in more participatory research, but an educator and activist exploring alternative paradigm research as one tool in the multifaceted struggles for a more just, loving world.

Pat Maguire

Contents

List of illustrations

Contributors

Carolyn Blackburn is an educational researcher and adviser. She was the project researcher for the FAS-eD Project and a project investigating Early Years Practitioners knowledge of FASD. Carolyn worked in childcare and education for 12 years as a researcher, adviser, Early Years' manager, family support worker, development worker and inclusion support worker. She is currently exploring the diverse communication needs of young children in the Foundation stage at Birmingham City University.

Barry Carpenter is Academic Director (Special Educational Needs) for The Schools Network. He holds the iNet International Chair for Special and Inclusive Education, as well as Honorary Professorships at the Universities of Worcester and Limerick. His post-doctoral research, at the University of Oxford, was in the education of children with FASD. In a career spanning 30 years, Barry has held the leadership positions of Headteacher, Chief Executive, Inspector of Schools, Principal Lecturer, and Director of the Centre for Special Education at Westminster College, Oxford. He lectures nationally and internationally.

Sally Conway has a background in Learning Disability Nursing and has worked in a variety of settings, supporting adults with learning disabilities. She is Head of Family and Student Services at Sunfield, a residential special school and charity in the UK offering education, care and therapies to children and young people with complex learning needs, aged between 6 and 19. Sally was instrumental in developing Family Services from its infancy in 1999 to the current high profile it holds within the organisation. She has undertaken extensive research regarding family issues which has served to shape and expand the service to continue to meet the wide and varying needs of all family members.

Jo Egerton is a Research Project Co-ordinator for the Schools Network, and has worked on the DfE-funded Complex Learning Difficulties and Disabilities Research Project. She had a consultative role in the NOFAS-UK supported FAS-eD project for children with Fetal Alcohol Spectrum Disorders. She has worked in the field of special educational needs for 14 years in residential care, education and research for students with severe and complex learning difficulties, and is currently working on the Schools Network's Research Charter Mark Award, supporting schools engaged in research. Her previous co-edited books include *New Horizons in Special Education and Early Childhood Intervention* (with Barry Carpenter), and *Moving with Research* (with Elizabeth Marsden).

Ann Fergusson is a Senior Lecturer in Special and Inclusive Education and a member of the Centre for Special Needs Education and Research (CeSNER) at the University of Northampton. Ann has been involved in research and consultancy projects for government, regional partnerships, local authorities, schools, independent and voluntary organisations in the UK and in some international contexts. With practitioners, she has developed training and resource materials to support schools and her work has been published in journals and books. She has also undertaken participative action research with children and young people and their teachers, in inclusive mainstream school and college settings.

Ann Gillies is a teacher of young children with labels of autism and a doctoral candidate at the University of South Florida. Ann has been teaching children with disabilities for 13 years and her research interests include inclusive education and listening to the voices of children. Ann has presented at conferences and been a visiting scholar in several different countries and is also interested in international perspectives on disability and practice.

Katherine Hawley is a doctoral student at the University of South Florida. She taught as a special education teacher before pursuing her Ph.D. in Curriculum and Instruction with an emphasis in Special Education. Katherine is also a teacher serving students with low-incidence disabilities in a secondary inclusionary setting. Her research interests are teachers' perceptions of alternate assessment.

Victoria Hobday is currently studying for a Doctorate in Clinical Psychology. She has a particular interest in the effects communication can have on emotional well-being, and completed the 'Voice for Choice' project while working as a Research Assistant at a residential school for children with severe learning disabilities and autism. This research led to the creation of a toolkit to promote and support choice-making in young people with learning disabilities.

Aisha Holmes is a doctoral student at the University of South Florida. She taught as a special education teacher before pursuing her Ph.D. in Curriculum and Instruction with an emphasis in Special Education. Her research focuses on the educational experiences of African American students.

Phyllis Jones is an Associate Professor in the Department of Special Education at the University of South Florida. Phyllis taught and was an administrator in schools in the UK for 15 years before she became a faculty member in the College of Education at Northumbria University. She is author of *Inclusion in the Early Years: Stories of Good Practice*, co-author of *Collaborate Smart*, and editor of *A Pig Don't Get Fatter the More You Weigh It: Classroom Assessment that Works* and *Leading for Inclusion: How schools can build on the strengths of all learners*. Phyllis has published widely in international journals related to inclusion, special education and teacher education. She is the Principal Investigator of the SAGE (Successfully Accessing General Education) OSEP grant that supports teachers to teach students with ASD and Severe Intellectual Disability labels in a least restrictive environment.

Christine Klopfer is a Special Education teacher in her fifth year of teaching students with autism in the Florida public school system. She has engaged in innovative collaborative teaching models that have been shared through the Center for Autism and Related Disabilities, has received Teacher of the Year honors for her second year teaching, and recently completed her master's degree in autism and low-incidence disabilities at the University of South Florida.

Teresa Whitehurst is a highly acclaimed Independent Consultant and Trainer focusing on the special educational needs sector and holding qualifications including MSc Clinical Neuropsychiatry, BSc Psychology and a post-graduate certificate in Research Methods. Teresa has published widely and regularly speaks at national and international conferences. She has worked with leading UK-based charities, mainstream and special schools and been involved with many international collaborations to develop leading edge practice. She worked for eight years as a researcher within a residential school for children and young people with severe and complex learning difficulties, supporting staff in extending, innovating and researching their practice.

Foreword

The time has never been more critical or crucial for our schools and for our education systems, to establish a culture of research that is school-based, classroom-focussed and child-centred. We need teachers who have as an integral part of their teaching repertoire the process of inquiry; teachers who are prepared to acknowledge openly that they do not know all of the answers to a child's learning needs. In so doing the teacher adopts a critical lens that enables them to explore, investigate, discover, for and with the student, what pedagogy, which curriculum, what experiences, will help that student to become an active, engaged participant in learning.

Why is this imperative so crucial now? We have reached a juncture in this twenty-first century where we can look back over the first decade and chart the dramatic changes in the child population. These have led to a new population of children with special educational needs and disabilities entering our school system. Often these are children whose needs are outside of the scope or previous experience of even the most skilled of teachers. A prominent example would be children born prematurely, particularly in very recent years, those who survive birth in the period 24–28 weeks. These children are often 'wired differently'; when they entered this world their brain structure was white matter, not grey matter; the cortical folding had not begun. If they survived in an incubator with intensive support, their brain would have continued to grow and develop, but the scaffolding may be different; it is an external brain, influenced and nurtured ex-utero. Hence different neuronal connections are made, messages are transmitted differently. Once in the classroom the key questions for teachers has to be 'If this child's brain is wired differently, in what way does he learn differently – and do I know? And when I do know something about his unique pattern of learning, in what ways will I teach differently?'

These major questions can only be explored in the context of what one school principal has described as a 'finding-out culture'. Even established university-based academics such as Dr Michael Guralnick in the USA, have acknowledged that we have a second generation of children with disabilities who are posing significant research questions, but that the resolution to these questions will be 'practitioner led and evidence based'. We have, in our schools, a new generation of children who need new generation pedagogy. There will be multiple causes for this, as commentators such as Blackburn and Whitehurst (2010) have indicated – intergenerational poverty, and modern medical progress. We could extensively debate, as teachers, those causes but ultimately it is the way we teach in response to the way the child learns that needs the most intensive debate. The child that enters through that classroom door today is the child I must educate to the best of my ability. I need information that helps me to appreciate in what ways the child's Fetal Alcohol Special Disorder will influence teaching and learning in my classroom. I do need to adapt and modify my teaching style to meet his personalised pathway of learning. This guidance has not always been forthcoming, leaving teachers 'pedagogically bereft' (Carpenter, 2011).

That is why this text edited by Phyllis Jones, Teresa Whitehurst and Jo Egerton is so timely. Through multiple trials, engaging teachers from a wide range of educational settings, they have developed the Accessible Research Cycle. Often research has been perceived as distant from the classroom; something to be undertaken in, or by, a university. For the holistic child needs articulated above, we have to let go of that thinking and bring research as a dynamic component into the daily ebb and flow of our classrooms. It is the vehicle by which, and through which, we will seek resolution to the challenges of pedagogy, inclusion and quality education posed by this twenty-first-century generation of learners. As the authors say, 'The concept of teachers as researchers needs to become part of our everyday language.'

A major issue for teachers in relation to research has always been the language it is couched in and the imponderable concepts which overarch it; this presenting insurmountable barriers. The opening chapter by Jones, Whitehurst and Hawley, dispels some of these myths, and constructs a case for teachers becoming 'the initiators and owners of the research'. Born of the Action Research paradigm and its now well-established use and effectiveness in education, the ARC offers a more participatory approach to classroom-based research, which truly addresses the teachers' research agendas, not one imposed externally. The subsequent chapters illuminate the Accessible Research in greater detail. Each chapter illustrates one of the eight key questions posed by the ARC, e.g. 'What has been said previously?', 'How am I going to share my discoveries?' The contributors, many of whom are school-based practitioners, powerfully articulate the journey of exploration and discovery they took, how the ARC guided them, and how they created in their classroom, school or workplace, a culture of inquiry. As such they became 'agents of change; ... reflective, strategic, investigative, inquiring practitioners'.

Schools are in a major transformational stage, organisationally and systematically. But at the heart of this transformation are children and the classrooms they inhabit. Teachers need support as they endeavour to develop a pedagogy built on Engagement (Carpenter et al., 2011); a pedagogy that will embrace all children inclusively as active, engaged participants in dynamic, creative learning experiences. This book exhorts teachers to own this process for themselves; a daunting prospect maybe but guided by inquiry as a major change agent then it becomes a possibility and (hopefully) a reality. Recent initiatives such as 'The Inquiry Framework for Learning' (http://complexld.ssatrust.org.uk), which emerged from the UK Department for Education-funded Complex Learning Disabilities and Difficulties project, clearly and practically illustrates the interface now between child need and pedagogical response. Inquiry is the change agent referred to in this book, and it is embodied in the Accessible Research Cycle. The ARC, in itself, is transformative, and thus resonates with the current change in education, at the same time giving teachers a tool for classroom-focussed transformation. In the words of Marcel Proust: 'The only real voyage of discovery consists not in seeking new landscapes, but in having new eyes.' I commend this text to you as you make your journey of discovery through accessible teacher-led research.

Barry Carpenter

References

Blackburn, C., and Whitehurst, T. (2010) Foetal alcohol spectrum disorders (FASD): raising awareness in early years settings, *British Journal of Special Education*, 27(3), 122–129.

Carpenter, B. (2011) Pedagogically bereft!: Improving learning outcomes for children with Foetal Alcohol Spectrum Disorders, *British Journal of Special Education*, 38(1), 37–43.

Carpenter, B., et al. (2011) *The Complex Learning Difficulties and Disabilities Research Project: Developing Pathways to Personalised Learning*. London: Specialist Schools and Academies Trust (now The Schools Network). [Online at: http://complexld.ssatrust. org.uk; accessed: 24.11.11.]

Acknowledgements

Together, the editors and their co-authors are grateful for the encouragement of Alison Foyle at Routledge for her continued support and counsel for the development of this book. Most importantly, we extend our deepest gratitude to teachers, administrators, students and their families who have participated in the inquiry projects discussed throughout the book, with whom we have had the good fortune to work, inquire and learn together – thank you.

Chapter 1

Reclaiming research

Connecting research to practitioners

Phyllis Jones, Teresa Whitehurst and Katherine Hawley

Introduction

Undertaking research within *any* setting by *any* practitioner can potentially be a very daunting experience. Adding a research dimension to an existing teaching role can be a challenge both in terms of capacity, resources and tools to undertake the task. However, the value of conducting research from the 'inside' is acknowledged as a valuable endeavour and that 'methodologies which support knowledge production from an insider perspective, at a localized level, are of great value in developing more nuanced and complex understandings of educational experiences, identities, processes, practices and relations' (Burke & Kirton, 2006, p. 2).

This book brings an inclusive lens to inquiry projects; a lens that aims to support the involvement of under-represented voices in research and promotes the idea that this is a valuable activity that will increase understandings of inclusive inquiry in classrooms and schools. It is acknowledged that there is a current continuum of delivery settings in schools that represent the most to least restrictive provision for students with disabilities. This book is intended to support practitioner inquiry along this current continuum of services with an explicit aim to encourage the development of more least restrictive experiences for all students. A Least Restrictive Environment (LRE) was highlighted in the US policy, the reauthorization of the Individuals with Disabilities Act (IDEA, 2004), which stated LRE means that:

> to the maximum extent appropriate, school districts must educate students with disabilities in the regular classroom with appropriate aids and supports, referred to as supplementary aids and services, along with their nondisabled peers in the school they would attend if not disabled.
>
> (IDEA, 20 U.S.C. §1412, 5, B)

It is envisioned that inquiry of the nature promoted through the Accessible Research Cycle (ARC) will lead to more meaningful inclusive experiences for students with disabilities and their families. This chapter describes the ARC, which forms the foundation of the book. The ARC is a research cycle that is intended to be understandable and meaningful for teachers while maintaining rigorous inherent research structures. The chapter begins by exploring the need for teacher research in an international perspective, introduces the cycle and explores how it supports practitioners to become researchers of their own practice. The chapter introduces subsequent chapters that discuss actual stories of practitioner research, gathered from practitioners in the UK and the USA. Each chapter is structured to allow the reader to first of all appreciate the content and process of the research project the practitioner has engaged with. Second, each chapter is developed to emphasize a particular stage of the ARC. Readers hear stories of each stage of the ARC in a developmental way; however, they may jump to specific chapters to gain information about a particular stage of the ARC. The penultimate chapter shares the responses of an international group of practitioners as they engage with the ARC, and the final chapter recaps on the role and potential of structured inquiry into practice as a way to improve teaching and learning for all students. Throughout the book we will refer to 'practitioner inquiry' to encompass the different professionals involved in the area of special education, including, but not limited to, teachers, families, speech and language, occupational therapists and physical therapists. However, we begin with an exploration of teachers as researchers, as this is where many of the roots of practitioner inquiry lie. This offers the reader a theoretical foundation of practice-based research that underpins the ARC.

Teachers as researchers: an international perspective

The concept of teachers as researchers has become part of our everyday language. In recent years, the profession has been charged to create a body of evidence-based practice to ensure teaching is informed, reflective and thoughtful. Hargreaves (1996) challenged researchers of teaching when he suggested that 'teaching could become an evidence-based profession only if researchers generated the kinds of evidence that teachers need; evidence focusing on teaching and learning, presented in useable formats, accessible and interesting to teachers' (quoted in Bell, Cordingley, Evans, Holdich, & Saunders, 2004, p. 3). It was in the 1980s that Stenhouse founded the concept of the 'teacher as researcher', although many years before Corey (1953) at Teachers College, New York, had involved teachers in 'active curriculum development' (Saha & Dworkin, 2009). Interest in meaningful practitioner research has been a mainstay of schooling since the early work of Corey. There has been a range of international initiatives that have emerged to assist in developing a 'more research-informed climate in educational practice' (Bell Cordingley, Evans, Holdich, & Saunders, 2004, p. 3). In the United Kingdom, Bell et al. discuss some of the initiatives, such as:

- the ESRC-funded teaching and learning research programme (TLRP);
- the development of systematic research reviews supported by the Evidence

for Policy and Practice Information and Co-ordinating Centre (EPPI Centre);
- the Department for Skills & Education Research Informed Practice (TRIPS) website;
- the General Teaching Council's Research of the Month (RoM) website;
- the development of the National Teacher Research Panel (NTRP).

In the United States, the federal law known as the No Child Left Behind Act (NCLB, 2002) has altered the role of teachers. NCLB (2002) mandates the use of data-driven interventions and holds teachers more accountable for student outcomes. Teachers have more responsibility in creating and implementing data-driven interventions within their own classrooms (Babkie & Provost, 2004). Indeed, teachers are expected to make professional decisions about the efficacy of evidence-based strategies in their classroom; they are expected to be reflective researchers of practice.

Some initiatives can be seen to assume that teachers and practitioners are *users* rather than *generators* of research, consuming research done within the world of academia rather than becoming a research-engaged profession. Others encourage teachers to create, interpret, share and rigorously evaluate practical evidence about teaching and learning in and for different contexts (Carpenter, 2007; Mertler, 2008). This research should be research which is conducted by those within educational settings as reflective and proactive practitioners.

The ARC offers a way to support teachers to generate and complete research about their own practice; thereby becoming the initiators and owners of the research. A set of key questions have been developed that supports teacher access to research and reflection on their own practice. Before introducing the ARC, the historical and powerful tradition of action research is discussed as a backdrop for the ARC.

Action research

Action research allows teachers to establish more personal relationships with their students while developing a deeper understanding of their students as learners (Rogers, Bolick, Anderson, Gordon, Manfra, & Yow, 2007). Action research is a practically orientated research methodology that can be defined as 'the process of studying a real school or classroom situation to understand and improve the quality of actions or instruction' (Johnson, 2005, p. 21). Burton and Bartlett (2005) note that action research was rooted in postwar problem solving utilizing a spiral of action involving fact-finding, planning and implementation. They advocate that action research could be employed in many settings to solve any number of professional problems, with education being a prime example. The methods of action research we are familiar with today are heavily influenced by the work of Lawrence Stenhouse who felt it essential that teachers 'reflected upon practice, shared experiences and evaluated their work' in order for the education of pupils to improve (Burton & Bartlett, 2005, p. 35; Saha & Dworkin, 2009). The process of action research allows a classroom teacher the opportunity to reflect on practice and develop a course of action based on an informed cycle of inquiry (Hartland, 2006).

An added benefit of action research is that it places practitioners in an active role in the school reform process (Brighton & Moon, 2007). There has been much written on action research and its structured process of inquiry, which allows a teacher ownership of the research process. Johnson (2005) offers descriptors of the action research process that shows how action research can be:

- systematic query-based;
- simple and clear to increase levels of rigour and effectiveness;
- well planned before collecting data;
- varied in length;
- involving regular and ongoing data collection;
- existing on a continuum;
- grounded in theory;
- including mixed research methodology.

Action research is cyclical in nature and intends to draw teachers into meaningful research about their practice. It is these fundamental principles of action research that have influenced the development of the ARC.

The Accessible Research Cycle (ARC)

However practical in nature action research is, any research method can often portray as a highly technical process and some teachers may be reluctant and possibly hesitant to participate in it. In reflecting upon a cycle of teacher research, as illustrated in Figure 1.1, we can see how the method may indeed appear overwhelming for some teacher researchers. For example, some of the language associated with research design and analysis may be off-putting and increase the likelihood of teachers leaving the research of teaching practices to others who appear more familiar with such technicalities. This should not be the case.

It is critical and beneficial for teachers to view themselves as capable inquirers into their own practice, thus the research process should be accessible but maintain high levels of rigour (Rinaldo, 2005). Figure 1.2 illustrates one way this can be achieved through the development of a series of main questions and subquestions that are infused into the traditional research cycle. The aim of these questions is to present research as a more familiar process; one that is attainable by practitioners living the life of teaching in classrooms and schools. Progressing through the cycle of Figure 1.2 by responding to the questions, teachers are supported to develop research into their own practice that is both thorough and meaningful. The questions have been designed to support teachers to engage in higher levels of analysis of their practice (Anderson & Krathwohl, 2000).

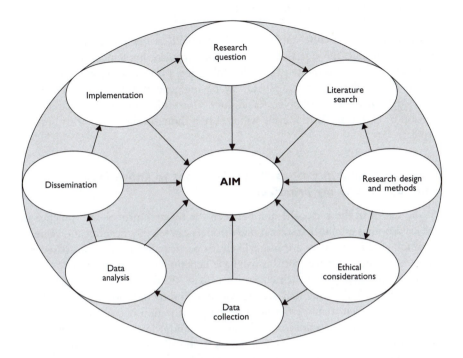

Figure 1.1 Cycle of teacher research

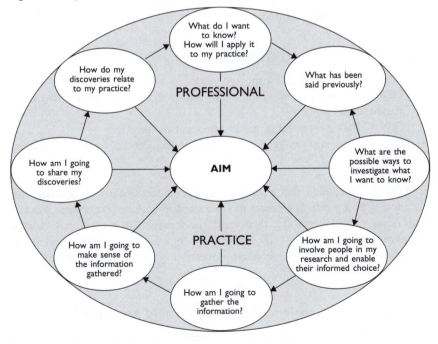

Figure 1.2 The Accessible Research Cycle

There are eight discrete stages to the Accessible Research Cycle. A practitioner proceeds through the questions at each stage to plan, implement and evaluate their research. It is suggested that when planning a project of inquiry, it will be helpful to plan the project in a global way, paying general attention to each of the stages to develop a holistic plan for inquiry. Once this is done, more careful attention to each stage of the cycle will ensure a thoughtful and rigorous inquiry project.

Stage One main questions: What do I want to know? How will I apply it to my practice?

At the outset of the cycle, the link between the research process and practice in the classroom is established so that practitioners can see the meaning and value of the inquiry. Practitioners are more likely to participate in classroom-based inquiry when they perceive that this will have benefits to their own practice and to the needs of the pupils in their classrooms (Rose, 2002). In the first stage, practitioners identify the issue they are interested in finding out more about, and this often occurs when they see the need to make a situation better. Questions that are more open in this 'definition' stage are 'how' and 'why' questions. Sometimes, practitioners may identify an issue and look for possible casual factors in order to frame question(s) they wish to explore in more depth (Schoen & Schoen, 2003; Schoen & Nolen, 2004). Professional reflection and questioning form a crucial element of practitioner research.

Sub-questions that support Stage One are:

- What is the knowledge I want to generate?
- How am I going to understand this knowledge in relation to my understandings and practice?
- How will any new insights impact my or others' practice?
- How will the knowledge gained contribute to a critical analysis of the key issues?

It is through this questioning phase that practitioners begin to appreciate how the inquiry process has the power to close the gap between theory and practice and become meaningful to them and their particular professional context (Brighton & Moon, 2007). By working through the main and sub-questions practitioners can develop a meaningful question or number of questions about their own practice.

Stage Two main question: What has been said previously?

In responding to the main question at Stage Two, the practitioner creates a sound evidence base for their research. Teaching has become an evidence-based profession where professional practice is firmly embedded in research (NCLB, 2002; General Teaching Council, 2006). Any research into classrooms and schools is a form of professional inquiry. Practitioners may use academic journals, professional journals, internet sources, and books that relate to the topic as ways to find out what has previously been done and said. This naturally enhances the credibility and the ultimate ability of the work to contribute to the knowledge base of current theories and practices about teaching and learning (Johnson, 2005).

Sub-questions that support Stage Two are:

- Where can I go to find out what has already been done in my area of interest?
- How am I going to make sense of the literature I find?
- How can I ensure that I am reading more than one perspective?

Stage Three main question: What are the possible ways to investigate what I want to know?

The third stage involves a question about how the project will be designed to gather the information the practitioner is interested in. Here, decisions are made about the nature of the research; is the research going to be quantitative, qualitative or a mixture of both methodologies? Later in the research cycle the practitioner chooses data gathering tools, where considerations involve more general approaches to inquiry. The nature of the question that emerged from Stage One, the research question, helps to determine meaningful methods. For example, a practitioner may want to examine test scores across an age group to find out how many students fit into particular levels of performance; this will call for data to be gathered about numbers of students at particular performance levels. In addition, the practitioner may also wish to gather insights from other practitioners about the particular tests used to generate the scores and may plan to adopt a survey and/or individual interviews. Blending quantitative and qualitative design methodologies has the potential to offer a more holistic perspective of an issue.

Sub-questions that support Stage Three are:

- Am I interested in finding out more about statistical data that may show trends and patterns in numbers? Positive responses to this may lead to quantitative approaches influencing the project.
- Am I interested in finding out more about real life stories and experience? Positive responses to this may lead to qualitative approaches influencing the project.
- Am I interested in finding out something about statistical patterns and

stories of experience? Positive responses to this may lead to a mixed method of approaches that influence the project.

Stage Four main question: How am I going to involve people in my research and enable their informed choice?

The main question at the fourth stage is concerned with the practical ways that practitioner researchers involve participants in the research process, considering both ethical and informed consent issues.

Sub-questions that support Stage Four are:

- Do I want all possible participants to have an equal chance of being selected in a random way?
- Do I want participants to volunteer because they are present at the time of the project?
- Do I want to choose participants as representative of the population?
- Do I want to have very specific, clear-cut criteria defined to identify potential participants?
- Do I want to hand-select participants due to characteristics that are ideal for my research project?
- Do I want to use a combination of the above questions in order to select my participants?

After deciding who to involve in the project, the next step is to ensure that all participants know about the research, appreciate how their involvement will benefit the research, their classroom or school, and know that their responses will be respected in a confidential and anonymous way. This is known as informed consent and provides one of the ways a practitioner researcher can explore ethical dimensions of the research (Orcher, 2005).

Additional sub-questions that support informed consent are:

- How can I tell my participants about the project in a simple but comprehensive way?
- How can I share with my participants the potential value of their involvement?
- How can I show my participants that their responses will be respected in a confidential and anonymous way?
- How can I share with my participants how I will protect them from any harm through the project?

In responding to these questions a practitioner researcher will create an ethical framework for their project of inquiry, one that safeguards the interests of the participants.

Stage Five main question: How am I going to gather the information?

Having decided upon the general approach to the research at Stage Three, the practitioner researcher is now supported to get into the detail of their research design responding to specific questions about the 'tools' to use to gather data. Data collection tools such as questionnaires, interviews, focus groups, reflective logs, checklists, video analysis, and observations are tools that a practitioner may choose to adopt to gather information. Schoen and Nolen (2004) remind us that for research to be meaningful and valid, it is important to generate data that links specifically to questions (that emerged at Stage One) and that are in keeping with the general research approach (chosen at Stage Three).

Sub-questions that support Stage Five are:

- Where can I find out simple and clear information about the range of tools I may use in my project?
- Who could I make connections with to help me decide which research tools I may use?
- How is the tool going to help me explore my question(s)?
- Will I need to include more than one tool? If so, how do the tools complement each other?

Stage Six main question: How am I going to make sense of the information gathered?

The main question at the sixth stage focuses upon the management and analysis of the collected data. It is at the analysis stage that many practitioner researchers become overwhelmed by the amount of data generated. It is crucial to help to manage the generated data to support meaningful analysis, and one way to overcome some of the difficulties in data management is to plan for the analysis process as early as possible in the inquiry project.

Sub-questions that support Stage Six are:

- How can I manage and organize the raw data in a way that makes sense to the practitioner researcher and the questions generated? For example, following a survey, the data could be sorted and gathered together into the survey 'prompt' sections.
- How can I interpret data (themes, shared experiences, feelings)? This is

where emerging themes are highlighted. For example, the use of colour-coded highlighting may be one way to achieve this.

- How can I ensure greater levels of validity? For example, posing the question, how true are the emerging themes? This question can be explored through sharing the data between practitioners and comparing the analysis.
- How can I ensure greater levels of reliability? For example, posing the question, did the generated data provide the area of insight that was intended?
- How can I potentially present results in a simple way that supports clear appreciation of the data and subsequent analysis?
- How can I present data in a way that shows my own meaning-making?
- Where are the links back to literature and do I need to carry out further literature searches?
- How can I present my data analysis in a way that relates the current findings and insights to my initial questions and also highlight the links to the literature base?

Stage Seven main question: How do my discoveries relate to my practice?

The linking of an inquiry project to practice is the essence of practitioner research. For an inquiry process to be ultimately meaningful it needs to inform current practice and hopefully influence decisions about what changes need to be made in the light of the findings of the project. For example, the project may have highlighted the need to design a new instructional practice or programme (Johnson, 2005).

Sub-questions that support Stage Seven are:

- How do the findings of this project inform my professional practice?
- How do the findings in this project inform the professional practice of others?
- How do the findings increase my understanding of children's responses?

It is through grappling with these questions that practitioners can be empowered with the necessary knowledge to bring about change in classrooms and schools.

Stage Eight main question: How am I going to share my discoveries?

At the eighth stage, practitioner researchers consider how to share discoveries from their inquiry project. Main and sub-questions at this stage relate to this process. Johnson (2005) suggests that practitioner colleagues could be the most appreciative audience for disseminating the findings of a project. Parents and families should also be included as these offer an audience with an invested interest in the inquiry. Other professional environments, such as professional conferences and conventions, academic journals, school district and local community organizations provide more general outlets for distributing findings (Johnson, 2005; Farrell & Weitman, 2007).

Sub-questions that support Stage Eight are:

- How will my colleagues best receive information about insights from my project?
- How will parents and students best receive information about insights from my project?
- How can I share with the wider profession the insights emerging from my project?
- What are my most comfortable ways of sharing information about my professional practice?
- In order to publish my project in a professional journal, what would I need to do?
- In order to publish my project in a peer-reviewed academic journal, what would I need to do?

Inquiry to support greater inclusive practices

There is a need for practitioner inquiry that is inclusive in nature. Inclusive inquiry can include projects that promote the gathering of understandings of meaningful inclusion across all educational settings. For example, it may highlight how a student with complex/severe disabilities can be a valued member of a whole school community or how the student with ADHD can be supported to be successful in the English class. Inquiry of this nature promotes the gathering and hearing of voices that may have been discounted or overlooked in past research (Fernandez, 2011; Head, 2011). Inclusive inquiry can bring change in developing more inclusive practices for those students who have differing and unique educational needs. Furthermore, it can enrich collaborative efforts that can led to more inclusive practices by establishing an inquiry culture in school through collaborative research partnerships (Argyropoulos & Nikolaraizi, 2009). The need and nature of inclusive inquiry are exemplified in the story embedded in Chapter 8.

Stories of practitioner research

Once the reader has become familiar with the ARC, the book progresses to share stories of practitioner research in the field of special and inclusive education that serve to highlight each of the above stages. In Chapter 2, Carolyn Blackburn shares her research on raising practitioner awareness of Fetal Alcohol Spectrum Disorders (FASD). Through sharing her story she highlights the first stage of the cycle and explores how the project helped her to explore the knowledge base amongst a group of practitioners relating to Fetal Alcohol Spectrum Disorders. This project provided a starting point for the design of a resource pack intended to equip practitioners with the knowledge to improve the quality of their support for children and families affected by FASD. Children affected by Fetal Alcohol Spectrum Disorders present a new and growing Early Childhood Intervention opportunity for Early Years Practitioners. In Chapter 3, Jo Egerton reveals how she explored the existing knowledge base in her project related to parents' views. Based on a UK project, 'From the Far Side' that explored how parents of young people with severe and complex learning disabilities viewed their son's or daughter's transition from school to adult services, this chapter describes what a literature review is, its purpose, and how Jo approached the task in her project on parents' views. The chapter emphasizes how a thorough literature review can identify key fundamental ideas, concepts and themes, identify the gaps in existing knowledge, and justify the need for the current research.

In Chapter 4, Sally Conway and Teresa Whitehurst guide the reader through the third stage of the ARC by sharing their efforts to lead trans-disciplinary UK-based research projects. They share the strategies they used to engage families in research. This collection of projects focuses upon the use of different strategies to undertake different types of projects when working with families. They discuss the considerations needed in a process that involves both families and multidisciplinary professionals in a research context and how these considerations impact the development of a project. In Chapter 5, Ann Gillies helps the reader to explore the fourth stage of the cycle by revealing how she approached informed consent in her US project with kindergarten children. Ann shares how achieving informed consent was complex and varied, differing according to the individual children in the project. The children were a diverse group: some were highly verbal; one was an emerging communicator; all had labels of 'autism', 'ADHD', 'language delay' or 'gifted'. The children were invited to participate in the project and were told about their participation in different ways and Ann shares the different tools she employed to support this. Chapter 6, based on a UK project 'Voice for Choice', follows the story of Victoria Hobday who guides the reader through Stage Five of the cycle and shares how she decided upon and employed a range of research tools. The Voice for Choice project was designed to explore how young people with Autism Spectrum Disorder (ASD) and mental health problems could be supported to make informed choices about their resources for interventions. The range of tools that Victoria employed includes: observations of the resources in various environments; feedback surveys from professionals; and direct interviews and activities with the young people themselves. In order to involve the young people, a range of communication methods were incorporated into the research design. Such communication methods were specific to an individual student's pattern of communication and included the use of symbols, photographs, picture exchange communication (PECS), Makaton, verbal communication and Talking Mats. Through the use of a variety of tools, Victoria shows how data collection was triangulated from a number of perspectives.

In Chapter 7, Katherine Hawley focuses upon Stage Six of the cycle and shares the strategies she employed to manage data that was generated through a US-based project on teachers' perspectives of Alternate Assessment. The study examined the perceptions of teachers of students with low incidence disabilities about a newly implemented State Alternate Assessment process (Florida Alternate Assessment; FAA) through the use of a survey (Likert-scale and open-ended questions). The chapter explores how the data was managed and analysed through coding and grouping in order to develop interpretations that remained true to the data and shed light on teachers' perceptions of how FAA impacted their work as practitioners. In Chapter 8, Christine Klopfer focuses on the seventh stage of the cycle and presents shared discoveries about US students' experiences of inclusive practices. The project was carried out at a Kindergarten through 8th grade public school in the South-West of Florida. It focuses upon an innovative way that research discoveries can be shared. The school had a district 'cluster' programme for children with autism. Following an inclusion project with general education students in the same grade range, a research project was designed to share the social growth of students with autism labels with the rest of the school. As part of this project, general education peers were interviewed about their experiences with the students with autism and explored how their perceptions about the students may have changed through spending time together. The interviews were videoed and a compilation of the interviews was created for dissemination. The video was shown across the school, in district meetings, and at a state conference. It was also posted on the Center for Autism and Related Disorders (CARD) website for global dissemination. In sharing discoveries, one lesson that emerged was the need to be opportunistic, be interesting, and be brief and simple to share. For the purposes of this research project, the medium of the video was ideal.

Chapter 9 relates to the final stage of the research cycle where Aisha Holmes shares her US-based student self-monitoring project and the impact that this project had on practice. Teachers often encounter behaviours that interrupt classroom instruction and learning. A technique implemented in this project was contingency-based self-monitoring. Contingency-based self-monitoring is an educational technique that involves students monitoring their own behaviour, for which they receive consequences that promote success (Hallahan & Kauffman, 2006). Self-monitoring or recording requires defining target behaviour, identifying functional reinforces, designing a self-monitoring tool, teaching the student the proper use of the tool, and fading the use of the tool. Fading the use of the self-monitoring tool should promote maintenance of acquired behaviours and skills over time, which ultimately generalizes to other settings and other behaviours (Polloway, Patton & Serna, 2005). This chapter shows how the use of contingency-based self-monitoring strategies in the classroom empowered students to take ownership of their own learning, which had a powerful impact upon the life of the classroom.

In Chapter 10, Phyllis Jones, Teresa Whitehurst and Jo Egerton, an inquiry project focused on practitioners' perceptions of the ARC is presented. As part of a professional development training using the ARC, practitioners from New Zealand completed a survey about their perspectives of the cycle. Four themes emerged from the survey: (1) confidence in themselves as researchers; (2) practical support in the research process; (3) generating ideas for research or benefits from practitioner research; and (4) de-mystifying the research process. These initial responses to the ARC show its promise to be helpful in the facilitation of practitioner-owned inquiry; practitioner research that aims to improve and change practice.

The final chapter, Chapter 11, considers how we embed research into classroom/school practice. In this chapter Ann Fergusson explores the historical and current perspective of the practitioner as a researcher and the constraints this places upon them. It looks in particular at such questions as:

- How has research in schools developed over the years?
- How have universities supported practitioner research?
- What contributes to the success of practitioner research in schools?
- Where does the future of research in schools lie?

Conclusion

Creating a research-informed profession within education empowers practitioners to become agents of change; they become reflective, strategic, investigative, inquiring practitioners. Creating ways to support meaningful inquiry into practice is crucial; this involves scaffolding the research process for practitioner researchers while ensuring the research is rigorous, reliable and valid. Developing main and sub-questions that facilitate practitioner access to meaningful research goes some way to remedying the differences which are perceived as insurmountable boundaries between the worlds of education and research (Saunders, 2007). Inclusive inquiry has the power to change inclusive educational practices for those with differing educational needs, to promote and highlight voices that have been underrepresented, and to assist in collaborative research endeavours (Argyropoulos & Nikolaraizi, 2009). An ARC, infused with jargon-free questions, has been presented as a helpful process to support practitioners who wish to inquire about their practice in an inclusive way. Facilitated practitioner research supports educators as producers of knowledge and makes them active participants in building the knowledge in their discipline. This, in turn, validates the role of the practitioner as both practitioner and researcher. As Whitehead (2004) states (cited in Carpenter & Egerton, 2007, p. 11): 'Research ... is not distant from practice but its lifeblood. It feeds the cycle of reflection, evidence, evaluation, teaching and learning. It's what excellent practitioners do.' It is now time to turn attention to how this looks in action.

References

Anderson, L.W., & Krathwohl, D.R. (2000). *A taxonomy for learning, teaching, and assessing: A revision of Bloom's taxonomy of educational objectives.* London: Allyn & Bacon.

Argyropoulos, V.S., & Nikolaraizi, M.A. (2009). Developing inclusive practices through collaborative action research. *European Journal of Special Needs Education, 24*(2), 139–153.

Babkie, A.M., & Provost, M.C. (2004). Teachers as researchers. *Intervention in School and Clinic, 39*(5), 260–268.

Bell, M., Cordingley, P., Evans, D., Holdich, K., & Saunders, L. (2004). What do teachers want from research and does the research address those needs? Paper presented at the Annual British Educational Research Association (BERA) Conference, Manchester Metropolitan University, Manchester.

Brighton, C., & Moon, T.R. (2007). Action research step-by-step: A tool for educators to change their world. *Gifted Child Today, 30*(2), 23–27.

Burke, P.J., & Kirton, A. (2006). The Insider Perspective: Teachers-as-researchers. *Reflecting Education, 2*(1), 1–4.

Burton, D., & Bartlett, S. (2005). *Practitioner research for teachers.* London: Paul Chapman Publishing.

Carpenter, B. (2007). Developing the role of special schools as research organisations: The Sunfield experience. *British Journal of Special Education, 34*(2), 67–76.

Carpenter, B., & Egerton, J. (2007). *New horizons in special education: Evidence-based practice in action.* Clent: Sunfield Publications.

Corey, S.M. (1953). *Action research to improve school practice.* New York: Teachers College Press.

Farrell, J.B., & Weitman, C. (2007). Action research fosters empowerment and learning communities. *Delta Kappa Gamma Bulletin, 73*(3), 36–45.

Fernandez, E. (2011). Child inclusive research, policy and practice. *Children and Youth Services Review, 33*(4), 487–489.

General Teaching Council for England (2006). *Using research in your school and your teaching: Research-engaged professional practice.* Available at: http://www.gtce.org.uk/publications/using_research/.

Hallahan, D., & Kauffman, J. (2006). *Exceptional learners: Introduction to special education (10th ed.).* Boston, MA: Pearson Education, Inc.

Hargreaves, D. (1996). Teaching as a research based profession: possibilities and prospects. The Teacher Training Agency Annual Lecture, Birmingham.

Hartland, C. (2006). Inquiry-based learning: Why? Where? How? *Reflecting Education, 2*(1), 5–18.

Head, B.W. (2011). Why not ask them? Mapping and promoting youth participation. *Children and Youth Services Review, 33*(4), 541–547.

Johnson, A. (2005). *A short guide to action research.* Boston, MA: Pearson Education.

Mertler, C.A. (2008). *Action research: Teachers as researchers in the classroom.* Thousand Oaks, CA: Sage.

Orcher, L. (2005). *Conducting research: Social and behavioral science methods.* Glendale, CA: Pyrczak Publishing.

Polloway, E.A., Patton, J.R., & Serna, L. (2005). *Strategies for teaching learners with special needs (8th ed.).* Upper Saddle River, NJ: Merrill/Prentice Hall.

Rinaldo, V. (2005). Today's practitioner is both qualitative and quantitative researcher. *High School Journal, 89*(1), 72–77.

Rogers, D., Bolick, C.M., Anderson, A., Gordon, E., Manfra, M.M., & Yow, J. (2007). 'It's all about the kids': Transforming teacher–student relationships through action research. *Clearing House, 80*(5), 217–221.

Rose, R. (2002). Teaching as a 'research-based profession': Encouraging practitioner research in special education. *British Journal of Special Education, 29*(1), 44–48.

Saha, L.J., & Dworkin, A.G. (2009). *International handbook of research on teachers and teaching.* New York, NY: Springer.

Saunders, L. (2007). Professional values and research values: from dilemmas to diversity. In A. Campbell and S. Groundwater-Smith (Eds.) *An ethical approach to practitioner research.* London: Routledge.

Schoen, S.F., & Nolen, J. (2004). Action research: Decreasing acting out behavior and increasing learning. *Teaching Exceptional Children, 37*(1), 26–29.

Schoen, S.F., & Schoen, A. (2003). Action research in the classroom: Assisting a linguistically different learner with special needs. *Teaching Exceptional Children, 35*(3), 16–21.

Whitehead, M., & Hartley, D. (2005). *Major themes in education: Teacher education.* London: Routledge/Taylor & Francis.

Legislation

Individuals With Disabilities Act (IDEA, 2004). Pub. L. 20 U.S.C. §1412, (5), (B).

No Child Left Behind Act of 2002, Pub. L. No. 107–110.

Chapter 2

What do I want to accomplish through my inquiry?

Raising practitioner awareness of Fetal Alcohol Spectrum Disorders

Carolyn Blackburn

Introduction

What is it I really want to know? This question is the first step in the Accessible Research Cycle (ARC). It goes beyond casual classroom thoughts into practitioner inquiry, and helps to frame the nature and scope of our project. It will lead to the fundamental questions that guide the inquiry – traditionally known as 'research questions'.

Different types of research question

Research questions are the 'engine which drives the train of enquiry' (Bassey, 1999, p. 67). They need to be strong and focussed, and running in the right direction! Meaningful inquiry into practice has research questions which are 'specific and doable' (Roberts-Holmes, 2005, p. 32). They need to be focussed enough on a specific area to be answerable in the time frame available. Research questions may be modified and/or replaced as the study develops, but without them the process of inquiry will be slow and chaotic (Bassey, 1999, p. 67). Roberts-Holmes (2005) points to two main types of questions in research that we can apply to our practice. The *overall questions* that frame inquiry will ideally:

- identify its limits and context;
- clarify its purpose;
- help to concentrate and focus thinking, reading and writing during the project;
- help to determine how to approach the project;
- keep it on course.

As the inquiry progresses there is a move away from the initial questions that frame inquiry to *field questions* that are more specific and detailed. These questions will help to answer the overall research questions by informing possible inquiry methods (see Chapter 6).

Background to the project

This chapter uses a case study approach to highlight the process of identifying a 'framing question' that is meaningful, objective, relevant and answerable, set in the context of early childhood care and education and special educational needs and disabilities (SEND). The project in question, entitled 'Building Bridges to Understanding', was a collaborative venture between an educational setting supporting children with Severe and Complex Learning Needs (SLD) and a Local Authority (LA) in the United Kingdom. It involved Early Childhood Professionals (ECPs) as co-researchers in investigating ECPs' knowledge of Fetal Alcohol Spectrum Disorders (FASD).

FASD is an emerging phenomenon in the UK, with a suspected prevalence of 1 in 100 children born every year (British Medical Association, 2007). Children affected can have facial differences and physical, learning and behavioural difficulties. The aim of the project was to raise ECPs' awareness and understanding of FASD and to design and implement a useful toolkit of resources which would enable and empower ECPs and other educators to support children and families in a meaningful and respectful way. Through the project, ECPs said they became conscious of their need to be informed about FASD, aware of the needs of children with FASD and their families, and more confident in their ability to support those needs.

Where do research questions come from?

Educators are continually challenged by classroom dilemmas that take them beyond their professional experience. There are two responses to this – either rising to these challenges and using them to extend knowledge and improve learning opportunities for the children and young people they teach, or turning away from them and narrowing their professional focus. Educators cannot be expected to hold the answers to every professional situation they encounter; however, in the ARC, they have a structure through which they can identify issues and actively explore possible solutions.

Fundamentally, research is about trying to discover something that was unknown before and communicating new knowledge to those who are interested, so 'uncovering and enabling the emergence of new understandings, insights and knowledge' (Rolfe and MacNaughton, 2010, p. 3). The people interested may be a class team, colleagues within a department or school, or practitioners outside the school. The topic of discovery may be something entirely new or something already known, but presented in a new context. It may begin informally with sharing concerns about a student's learning with colleagues, and from a number of perspectives, for example:

- everyday professional practice;
- observations of children and young people in a range of contexts and environments;

- discussions with families/other professionals/colleagues/wider stakeholders;
- continuing professional development/training.

Once the area for discovery is identified, an investigation of what is already known about the topic helps to identify any important issues and current gaps that the project will explore in more detail (see Chapter 3). These can be referred to as potential 'inquiry paths'. A number of possible inquiry paths may be generated, but the practitioner researcher must focus on a specific strand of interest to ensure that any inquiry is achievable and 'doable'.

FASD Building Bridges project: first steps

The National Organisation on Fetal Alcohol Syndrome (NOFAS-UK), the school's director of research and the LA were very concerned about the lack of educator knowledge of FASD and successful educational strategies for the students affected by it. Early discussions led to initial overall questions: 'How many educators know about FASD?' and 'What can we do to increase their knowledge?' However, to answer these very broad initial questions would have been beyond the resources of the organisation in terms of finance, time, and staffing. It was therefore necessary to focus the project within a realistic scope.

In the real world: identifying constraints

A common mistake when starting an inquiry is to make the research question too big to be completed. It is important to keep the inquiry within the bounds of what is possible. In other words, can it be meaningfully completed within constraints of the inquiry (Cohen, Manion and Morrison, 2007)? These constraints may include, but are not limited to:

- availability of participants and co-researchers – and external settings if relevant;
- project ownership – the school, any research partners or funders may have specific ideas or outcomes which need to be included or negotiated, and about responsibilities for dissemination;
- potential cost;
- available time and timescales – what needs reprioritizing to make the research achievable?; what are the deadlines?
- any sensitive issues related to intended recipients of the project outcomes;
- ethical considerations – practitioners have a responsibility to ensure that inquiry is respectful to the people they involve (e.g. it acknowledges their privacy and dignity) and reflects the principles of democracy and truth (Bassey, 1999) (see Chapter 5); this is especially true when inquiry involves vulnerable groups in society, such as young children and those with Special

Educational Needs and Disabilities (SEND), as was the case with the research project discussed in this chapter;

• the impact of policy and guidance – at school, organization or government level.

FASD Building Bridges project: considering constraints

The initial broad research questions identified for the FASD Building Bridges project were reconsidered in the context of the contextual constraints by a team of practitioner researchers. This was done in collaboration with the Research and Ethics Committee at the school and a focus group, which included members of the LA and ECPs. The members of the Research and Ethics Committee included, among others, the school's chief executive/Research Institute director, a senior lecturer from a local university education department, a school governor with responsibility for research, and the research and development officer, who supported staff involved in research projects across the residential school. Members of the focus group from the LA included the Children's Services service development manager, the inclusion manager, two nursery integration workers, and an area special educational needs coordinator (SENCo). The ECPs represented leaders and SENCos from a range of settings including sessional pre-schools, private day nurseries and children's centres. There were a number of constraints to the project that included issues relating to access, source of funding, and timescale and budget.

Access

The availability of educators for interviews, discussion, evaluation of resources, and attendance at focus group meetings affected what was possible to achieve within the time period for the project.

The source of funding

The Early Years and Childcare Service for an LA in the UK funded the study; therefore, the study had to be contextualized within the early childhood sector in the county for which that LA was responsible, and to relate directly to children from birth to 5 years of age and their families. This decision to adopt an early years focus was supported by 'What people had said previously' in literature. Guralnick states that there is 'unequivocal evidence that the declines in intellectual development that occur in the absence of systematic early intervention, can be substantially reduced by interventions implemented and evaluated during the first 5 years of life' (2004, p. 13).

FASD is also identified as an under-researched area of both early childhood practice and SEND (Ryan and Ferguson, 2006; Carpenter, 2011).

Timescales and budget

The LA stipulated that the study must be completed within a specified budget and an agreed timescale. This had implications for how many hours of the researchers' time could be employed, and how many ECPs could be included in the study, allowing for the researchers' time for interview and analysis of data, as well as writing up of results.

Establishing aims, objectives and research questions

Once any constraints have been explored, the inquiry can be refined within the context of these issues. This sets the scene for identification of what will be accomplished through the inquiry (aims and objectives) from which the research questions can evolve. This step is the translation of a very general research aim or topic into specific, concrete researchable questions, which indeed can often be the most challenging part of the research development. Rolfe and MacNaughton (2010) suggest the specification of a set of operations or behaviours which can be measured, addressed or manipulated. This process of 'operationalization' transforms the general overall research questions into particular, specific research questions which relate to the real-life situation. This can also be viewed as moving from an abstract conceptual question to a more concrete one.

FASD Building Bridges project: aims, objectives and research questions

The process of drawing up detailed aims and objectives for the research project helps to identify the overall research questions. The Building Bridges study had four overall aims:

1 To establish best practice in supporting young children with FASD.
2 To develop a set of resources to enhance ECP knowledge and skills to facilitate working with children with FASD.
3 To develop a one-day training course and materials suitable for internal and external training.
4 To introduce best practice into early years settings relating to the education and support of children with FASD.

These aims were underpinned by four objectives:

1 To establish an ECP Focus Group to ensure the development of resources and literature are rooted in the practitioner perspective.
2 To develop resources to meet the needs of ECPs working in a variety of settings to support young children with FASD.

3 To conduct a literature review around best practice in the support of children with FASD in early years settings.
4 To develop a training course to support educators.

Working from the project's aims and objectives, the overall questions relating to educators' knowledge of FASD and their related practice were broken down into questions, which could be answered in a concrete manner. The specific research questions resulting from these aims and objectives were:

• What is the current best practice for working with young children with FASD?
• What resources could be developed to support educators working with young children with FASD?
• How can this knowledge and practice be effectively disseminated?

The research question in the Building Bridges project was directly relevant and meaningful to the educators, families and children for whom the LA had a duty of care.

It was felt that these aims, objectives and specific questions were relevant, purposeful and achievable in the time frame (12 months) and budget limitations allowed for the project.

Maximizing the relevance of the inquiry

In Chapter 1, it was established that practitioners are more likely to participate in classroom-based inquiry when they perceive that this will have benefits for their own practice and the needs of the pupils in their classrooms (Rose, 2002). However, if the inquiry can also reflect organizational and perhaps national aims and objectives, its relevance and impact will be greater. One way to maximize such relevance is to make sure the research question is set within the legislative context. In the United States, the types of educational services provided to young children with disabilities are specified by legislation (Cook, Tessier & Klein, 2000); for example, the need to adopt evidence-based practices. In the UK, the legislation is less prescriptive (Long, 1996; Roffey, 1999), although a general educational framework governs some practices (Porter, 2002). The current statutory SEN Code of Practice (Department for Education and Skills, 2001), which sets the context for setting-based inquiry for educators in terms of identifying, assessing and meeting the special educational needs of children, is undergoing significant revision. It will be interesting to see how educator inquiry is supported within the new guidance that replaces it.

Another way of increasing the relevance of the research question is by involving people who have an interest in the project (e.g. students, families, professionals, other stakeholders) in developing the research question. From their different points of view they often have insights that increase the value and usefulness of the research.

The Building Bridges project: involving stakeholders

The LA have a duty of care and interest to ensure that the early years settings registered with them provide quality of care and education for the children and families accessing their provision (Department for Education and Skills, 2001, pp. 8–9). Therefore, the aims of the project and research outcomes were identified together with key members of the LA and also professionals from the educational settings taking part in the research. At the end of the project, findings would be communicated to those who plan the resource and training needs of ECPs within the LA, as well as to the educators themselves. Research has more impact if it directly relates to their current interest and concerns.

It is important to note here that the relationship between funders and researchers must be mutually respectful. Cohen et al. (2007) remind us that while funders have the right to expect high quality, rigorous and usable research, they should not put the researcher in a position where the nature and ethical standards of the research are compromised. In the case of the Building Bridges project, the purpose of the outcomes was clearly defined by the LA with ECPs in mind. The school based research and ethics committee guided the nature and method of inquiry. (For more discussion on the importance of the research and ethics committee, see Chapter 5.)

Exploratory scoping to shape research questions

Bassey finds that the best way to think about the area of inquiry is to see it as an issue to be explored, a problem to be tackled or a hypothesis to be tested (1999, p. 66). This then provides a platform for framing the research questions.

The Building Bridges project: scoping using questionnaires

In the FASD Building Bridges study, an initial scoping survey which was carried out among early years settings to discover the level of educator knowledge about FASD revealed that the majority (78%; n = 161) of settings stated they knew nothing or very little about FASD, and felt that they would be ill prepared to plan for this group of children without relevant training (Blackburn, 2009; Blackburn and Whitehurst, 2010). The fact that, other than such general observations, these questionnaires showed no specific recommendations for problems to be solved or hypotheses to be tested relating to educators' knowledge of FASD reflected the lack of knowledge of FASD among the group interviewed. Thus the questionnaire outcome could best be viewed as an imperative to focus on the issue of the support of young children with FASD in early years settings, through a process of asking pertinent and relevant questions of educators relating to the issue.

The ethics of research questions

Roberts-Holmes (2005, pp. 57–58) recommends that the following questions are answered in consideration of ethical issues in early childhood research:

- What potentially sensitive issues are raised by the research questions?
- What are the various ways in which the research questions might be inadvertently taken the wrong way?
- How might your questions cause the research respondent to worry in any way after you have finished?
- Could the research questions inadvertently have any negative impact upon relationships within the early childhood institution?
- Could the research questions inadvertently have any negative impact upon family relationships?
- In what ways does the research make the setting and its members vulnerable to potential criticism?
- What advantages to the respondents and their early childhood settings might there be from the research?

It is important to consider these points to make sure that a research question is ethically sound. If there is any possibility that it is not, this should be discussed with someone experienced in research (e.g. at the education department of a local university), and the question changed if necessary.

The Building Bridges project: ethical considerations

Educators rely on a successful partnership with families in order to provide a quality care and learning experience for the children in their settings. Any project that involves educators as co-researchers must respect this close relationship and pay particular attention to ethical considerations, particularly where children with SEND are involved and stigma may surround a particular condition. As FASD is a disability that relates to maternal alcohol consumption, one of the most important ethical considerations for this particular project was the potential impact that ECPs' awareness of the cause of FASD might have on their typically supportive role with families. The research question was carefully designed to avoid asking educators to diagnose FASD or place any judgement or suggestion of stigma on parents of children with FASD, and in particular biological parents. Hence, the research question related strictly to educators' knowledge, current support strategies for children and families and future training and resource needs. In this way, the study avoided putting educators in a position that compromised their necessarily close partnership with families. The accuracy and robustness of the research question and the way it was communicated to educators in this respect were crucial to positive research outcomes. One ECP commented on this in the final evaluation of the Resource Pack produced at the end of the project: 'It's good that the emphasis is not on diagnosis' (Blackburn, 2009, p. 32).

Reframing the study in the light of initial findings

Initially it was hoped that the project would locate children in early years settings who had a diagnosis of FASD, so that the resources developed could be trialled with those particular children, refined and finalized to form evidence-based materials. However, this was not the case, although three of the 33 educators interviewed had knowingly supported a child with FASD in previous settings, and one setting was supporting a child who was being assessed for diagnosis at the time of the research. From evidence in the literature, it was thought that this could be due to the recognized under-diagnosis of FASD (Mukherjee, pers. comm., 2009). It was necessary, therefore, to re-frame the research methodology to reflect this. The aims, objectives and questions remained unchanged; however, the emphasis of the study moved to the need to raise awareness about FASD and provide a useful, practitioner-developed resource pack and training opportunities to support educators in their work with children with FASD and their families.

Relating research outcomes back to the research question

Research questions guide the research all the way through the project, keeping it on track, influencing what information is collected and how it is analysed. It is therefore very important that the stated research outcomes relate to the research questions.

The Building Bridges project: how the research question relates to different areas

As mentioned above, an initial survey was mailed to a range of educational settings (specifically those providing for children aged birth to 5) in a county in the UK. Of 400 settings, 161 replied (40%). A participant group of providers (33 settings in total) was selected from those who responded to this survey to take part in semi-structured interviews. The group was chosen to include as many as possible of the different types of early years setting operating within the county. In addition, a set of information sheets and supportive inclusion materials were developed from knowledge within the research team and information provided by educators who responded to the initial survey. These materials were trialled amongst the 33 settings, further refined following their response to an evaluation of the materials, and made available to educators across the county.

The initial survey asked about educators' existing knowledge about FASD and their confidence in supporting a child with FASD and their family; whether they had supported a child with FASD either in their current setting or a previous setting; what types of special educational needs they were currently supporting in their settings; and the effective inclusion strategies that had been useful for them that they would like to share with other educators. Educators were also asked about the type and availability of resources and training they thought would be most effective to enable their support of children with FASD and their families based on the knowledge the project had provided them with. The interview schedule was designed to explore: knowledge about FASD in more detail; educators' knowledge about SEND generally; inclusion strategies used by a range of educators in a variety of settings; and barriers to inclusion for young children with FASD.

Information from the responses to the initial survey, interviews with educators, evaluations of the materials and discussions resulting from the ECP Focus Group meetings, and Project Steering Group Meetings, were analysed by theme in a Project Report which could be used to inform future inclusion policy and practice within the LA. The results from the project can be related back to the original research questions in a number of ways outlined below using each question as a heading.

What is the current best practice for working with young children with FASD?

As none of the educators participating in the study was currently supporting a child with FASD in their setting, this question was answered mainly from an exploration of the literature. However, three educators had previously supported a child with FASD, and one ECP was supporting a child who was being assessed for diagnosis at the time of the study. These educators were able to give a view of what *might* be supportive based on the information provided to them from the project about the particular needs of children with FASD in the early years. Educators stated that best practice in supporting children with FASD in their early years would seem to rest on the basic principles of consistency, simplicity, structure, repetition, routine, constant supervision and valuing the child for their achievements and strengths (Blackburn, 2009). This is affirmed by Kleinfeld and Wescott (1993, p. 319) who state: '[Children with FASD need] special pre-schools where teachers carefully supervise children all the time, routines are clear and unvarying, classroom spaces are clearly marked and visual information supplements verbal directions'.

Carpenter (2011, p. 2) agrees, finding that: 'classroom accommodation, adaptation and amelioration are required to engage children with FASD as effective learners' and that high levels of engagement in learning are observed when tasks and language are broken down into small steps, routine provides predictability and curricula is personalized around the child's strengths (Blackburn, 2010).

What resources could be developed to support educators working with children with FASD?

All of the educators who participated in an interview stated that they would like further information and access to training opportunities relating to FASD. Their preferences for the type of information included:

- information about FASD, symptoms and signs to look for, how it affects children's learning, and how it affects families;
- strategies for supporting young children affected by FASD;
- specific activities designed to support young children affected by FASD;
- information they can pass on to other professionals, such as Health Visitors, to inform them about FASD.

The Resource Pack resulting from the study incorporated these preferences from educators and thus became a resource designed by educators for educators.

How can this knowledge and practice be effectively disseminated?

The type, format and timing of training preferred by educators were reasonably consistent across the range of settings involved in the project. Nearly all of the settings (93%) stated that early evening would be the best time for training, as finding cover for staff absence during the day can be difficult and the need to maintain adult-to-child ratios can restrict the number of staff who can attend any one session. Some of the LA-maintained nurseries stated that a late afternoon session at approximately 4.30–6.30 p.m. would be helpful, but most practitioners, and particularly childminders said that they could not attend training before 7.00–7.30 p.m. in the evening. Educators felt that a session lasting 2–3 hours would be adequate for the purpose. Some educators suggested that training could take place at Early Years Conferences, Early Years Providers Forums, Children's Centres (Integrated Services) or be setting based, although they appreciated that this might be difficult from a practical and cost viewpoint.

Raising awareness about FASD among educational professionals was the overarching aim of the study and was achieved throughout the project by the project team members disseminating information at a number of early years forums, training events relating to FASD, and newsletters produced by the LA for providers. A one-day conference was also held in the county at the end of the project in order to share findings with a range of professionals from health, social care and education. The materials developed from the study are available as an Educational Resource Pack and free to download from both the LA and school websites (see reference section: Blackburn, 2009). This allows the knowledge and practice developed from the study to be implemented across a geographically wide range of educational settings.

Conclusion

This chapter has highlighted the importance of the quality, clarity and robustness of the aims, objectives and subsequent questions of a project of inquiry. This will help ensure positive outcomes, not only for the study in question, but also for the participants of the study. The FASD Building Bridges project has highlighted the importance of educators being involved in research studies such as this in order to improve their inquiry-based professional approach to Early Childhood Intervention. Educators will then be in an ideal position to 'intervene at the point at which their interventions can pre-empt, or lessen the impact of emerging difficulties' (Carpenter, 2005, p. 14) for children in emerging areas of SEND, such as FASD.

The project also highlighted that research questions must be capable of being answered in the light of any contextual issues impacting the project, such as time and cost and access to particular groups of children or other participants. There must be flexibility within the study for the questions to be modified where necessary so that the study responds to emerging themes from the information gathered.

References

Bassey, M. (1999) *Case Study Research in Educational Settings*. Maidenhead: Open University Press.

Blackburn, C. (2009) *Building Bridges with Understanding: Foetal Alcohol Spectrum Disorders (FASD) Project: The Acquisition of Early Years Practitioner Knowledge in Relation to the Education and Support of Children with Foetal Alcohol Spectrum Disorders.* Worcestershire: Worcestershire County Council. Available at: www.sunfield.org.uk/ research_projects.htm/www.worcestershire.gov.uk/cms/education-and-learning/ enjoy-and-achieve/early-years-and-childcare/information-for-providers/fasd.asp (accessed 21 Feb. 2011).

Blackburn, C. (2010) *Facing the Challenge and Shaping the Future for Primary and Secondary aged Students with Fetal Alcohol Spectrum Disorders.* Available at: http:// www.nofas-uk.org/news.htm#tdanews (accessed 18 Feb. 2011).

Blackburn, C. and Whitehurst, T. (2010) Foetal alcohol spectrum disorders (FASD): raising awareness in early years settings, *British Journal of Special Education*, 27(3), 122–129.

British Medical Association (2007) *Fetal Alcohol Spectrum Disorders: A Guide for Healthcare Professionals.* London: British Medical Association.

Carpenter, B. (2005) Real prospects for early childhood intervention, family aspirations and professional implications. In Carpenter, B. and Egerton, J. (eds) *Early Childhood Intervention: International Perspectives, National Initiatives and Regional Practice.* Coventry: West Midlands SEN Regional Partnership.

Carpenter, B. (2011) Pedagogically bereft!: Improving learning outcomes for children with Foetal Alcohol Spectrum Disorders. *British Journal of Special Education*, 38(1), 37–43.

Cohen, L., Manion, L. and Morrison, K. (2007) *Research Methods in Education.* Abingdon: Routledge.

Cook, R.E, Tessier, A. and Klein, M.D. (2000) *Adapting Early Childhood Curricula for Children in Inclusive Settings*, 5th edn. New Jersey: Merrill.

Department for Education and Skills (DfES) (2001) *Special Educational Needs Code of Practice*. Nottingham: DfES Publications.

Guralnick, M. (2004) Effectives of early intervention for vulnerable children: a developmental perspective. In Feldman, A., *Early Intervention: The Essential Readings*. Oxford: Blackwell Publishing.

Kleinfeld, J. and Wescott, S. (eds) (1993) *Fantastic Antone Succeeds! Experiences in Educating Children with Fetal Alcohol Syndrome*. Fairbanks, AL: University of Alaska Press.

Long, P. (1996) Special educational needs. In Robson, S. and Smedley, S. (eds) *Education in Early Childhood: First Things First*. London: David Fulton.

Porter, L. (2002) *Educating Young Children with Special Needs*. London: Sage.

Roberts-Holmes, G. (2005) *Doing Your Early Years Research Project: A Step-by-Step Guide*. London: Sage.

Roffey, S. (1999) *Special Needs in the Early Years: Collaboration, Communication and Coordination*. London: David Fulton.

Rolfe, S.A. and MacNaughton, G. (2010) Research as a tool. In MacNaughton, G., Rolfe, S.A. and Siraj-Blatchford, I. (eds) *Doing Early Childhood Research: International Perspectives on Theory and Practice*. Buckingham: Open University Press.

Rose, R. (2002) Teaching as a 'research-based profession': encouraging practitioner research in special education. *British Journal of Special Education*, 29(1), 44–48.

Ryan, S. and Ferguson, D.L. (2006) On, yet under, the radar: students with Fetal Alcohol Syndrome Disorder. *Exceptional Children*, 72(3), 363–365.

Chapter 3

What has been said before?

Stand tall on the shoulders of giants

Jo Egerton

Introduction

So you have no time to read? Even if you think you don't, do not be tempted to skip this chapter! Finding out what others have said may be easier than you think, and can save a lot of time, energy and errors. As with every aspect of the Accessible Research Cycle (ARC), it is important to recognise that reading will be squeezed into an already hectic professional schedule and needs to be do-able while being of value. Once the research question is finalised, the next phase in the ARC is to find out about what other people have written about the chosen topic. This can seem a daunting task, and with so much information in circulation, it is good to be able to narrow it down and take some short cuts!

The aim of this chapter is to help establish firm foundations on which to base the inquiry. It is well said that those who do not know history are condemned to repeat it. Conversations with knowledgeable colleagues generate ideas and help avoid pitfalls. Learning more about a chosen inquiry area can lead to different angles and approaches. To illustrate key points in this chapter, examples are used from 'From the Far Side' – a research project that explored how parents of young people with severe and complex learning disabilities perceived their son's or daughter's transition from school to adult services.

Finding out what others have said

Contrary to what many people think, finding out what others have said about an area of interest is not a case of reading everything ever written on the subject, nor does it mean picking up the first few professional magazine articles that come to hand. Its main purposes are to discover:

- the main current developments and arguments;
- the important things key people have said;
- how this relates to the inquiry;
- the best way of approaching the inquiry;
- the mistakes that others have made and how to avoid them.

By the end of this chapter, the reader will know:

- how to focus their reading;
- what the range of different literature available is and how to access it.

The information given in this chapter, and the approach described, allow practitioners to gain a quick overview of reading to support practical research in the classroom. However, this will not be at the level needed to support a research-based qualification. Reading at qualification level would need to be more systematic and comprehensive. Those who would like to take a more in-depth approach to their reading will find many suitable sources (e.g. Aveyard, 2010; Hart, 1998).

Taking stock

Practical inquiry takes place in the real world, and it is important to recognise that time, people and resources are in limited supply. Lawson (2007, p. 8) wisely advises: 'Don't feel that you have to read everything. For a small-scale study you may not need more than half a dozen key texts.'

The busy practitioner beginning an inquiry has to plan carefully and realistically. It is important to know what is intended to be achieved by the end of the reading, to be specific in what will be read and to collaborate with others. If the original plan is not workable, the time period should be adjusted and/or new work priorities agreed.

Reading to support practical inquiry will include finding out:

1 what others have written about the topic of interest;
2 the best way to collect evidence;
3 the best way of using it to demonstrate outcomes.

As points 2 and 3 are covered in Chapters 6 and 7, the focus of this chapter will be point 1 – reading in relation to the topic of interest.

The purpose of reading about an inquiry topic is to lay the foundations and boundaries of the inquiry, to identify how it fits with what others have found out to date, and the added benefits the new inquiry will bring. In doing this, the practitioner will need to do the following:

- Define the key words in the research question (discussed in greater depth on pages 34–35) so that they and others know exactly what they are talking about.
- Find out about relevant government policy and guidance.
- Read relevant, recent books and articles – so they are aware of the main thinking and discussions around their topic, and what respected specialists in the field think.
- Find out what best practice, including evidence based practices, is in the area.

- Work out how the inquiry relates to what has gone before and the value of the planned outcomes.
- Make a list of what they have read.

In carrying out a literature review, and throughout the research process, it is important for the practitioner to see themselves as part of a community of researchers all learning from each other, building on each other's ideas and contributing to shared knowledge and improved practice to the benefit of the students they work with. Although for busy, practically motivated practitioners, it might seem easier to reinvent the wheel rather than reading what others have done before them, often wheels which have already been invented and refined run more smoothly, and will ultimately cause less trouble, leading to more successful outcomes (Constable, pers. comm., 2011).

Starting from where you are

The first step in undertaking inquiry is to stop … and take a good look round at people in the professional or local community. Who else around knows about and has an interest in the chosen topic? Whose work will affect the inquiry – teaching staff, parents, the young people involved, therapists, catering staff, psychologists or others? Who has experience in research? Does the school principal or another colleague have a useful contact at a local college or university who can give advice? Talking to colleagues and others is worth doing. For a start, it will help begin the inquiry! It can also save time. It may generate ideas not yet thought about, offer pointers towards useful reading, create opportunities for working with others, give ideas for reducing workload, and suggest different approaches, potential difficulties, and useful contacts.

This would be a good time to begin an 'inquiry journal'. The practitioner should keep *dated* notes of the interesting points and outcomes of these and future conversations, so they can go back to them and chart the developments of their research over time. With other pressures, it is easy to misremember or forget and the journal helps as an *aide-mémoire*!

Sharing the load

Within the context of a busy school day, making time for reading will be difficult with all the other competing concerns. It is often easier, and more enjoyable, if practitioners can share this with others. Maybe each person in a small group could commit to identifying and reading a paper which is relevant to the inquiry topic, and then meet to report on and discuss them (Constable, pers. comm., 2011). Perhaps, if the inquiry topic is of school-wide importance, this could be done within a staff focus group (McGill, 2010) or as part of a staff meeting.

Defining terms

Both the practitioner leading the inquiry and others need to be clear about what the terms used in the research question actually mean. The first danger is that, unless there is a written definition, over the course of the inquiry, those involved can gradually change the meaning of the word without realising it, so that the evidence collected during the inquiry is inconsistent. If this happens, the outcomes of the inquiry will be meaningless, and all the hard work wasted. A second danger is that colleagues can become confused by what the words actually mean. When this happens, misunderstandings can arise. Taking the research question, it is helpful to ask about the key words, 'What do I mean by this word? Can someone else possibly think it means something different?' If the answer to the second question is 'Yes', the term needs to be defined. Asking a range of different people what they think the term means is useful and revealing. To illustrate this, here is an example from 'From the Far Side'.

The main research question for the 'From the Far Side' inquiry was:

> What are parents'/guardians' perceptions of the importance of sharing information between a residential school and adult residential placements to support post-school transition for their son/daughter with severe learning disabilities?

Although this seems a bit of a mouthful, being very specific about what is being done during an inquiry makes the inquiry focused and achievable within a time frame and busy schedule.

Before reading further, look at the research question again in detail, and list the words or phrases which could be ambiguous. Then compare this with the list of terms defined in the literature review for the 'From the Far Side' research:

- Sharing information – does this mean written or verbal information; information shared formally or informally; or all of these?
- Transition – there is a lot of writing about post-school transition; in this case, does this mean transition to adulthood in the broadest sense or only a physical transition between environments?
- Severe learning disabilities – there is a wide range of definitions of severe learning disabilities (including legal definitions) nationally and internationally; which one applies in this research?

The good news is that specialists and researchers writing about a topic of interest have put a lot of thought into how to describe or define key terms. They will have thought through and debated their definitions in a way that a practitioner is unlikely to have time to do. When reading about their topic, knowledge about how others have defined key terms will be gained. These can then be used or adapted in an inquiry project. It is important to acknowledge the book or article in which the original definition appeared (see 'References' section) and to say how and why it was changed.

Tracking down relevant reading

With limited time to search out the most important books and papers and to read them, it is important to know how to find them relatively quickly, and to make sure that what is read matches the three Rs – relevant, recent and reputable. Again, it helps to talk to people with expertise. In addition to recommendations from personal professional contacts described above, practitioners can find help from:

- relevant professional or charitable organisations;
- the library of their nearest university with an education department;
- the internet.

The aim of this extended search is to identify the most important, reputable and up-to-date sources of information to support an inquiry. However, before this happens, it is essential to know the topic of the inquiry, the research question, and the key search words.

Identifying search words

Search words are commonly the key words or phrases within the main research question which can be used to find relevant reading – usually using the internet or electronic databases. Using search words enables practitioners to make an initial assessment of the usefulness of a piece of writing. In electronic searches, the computer will match the search words with words appearing in books and articles. It is important to make the search words specialised enough, so that the search does not produce a mountain of irrelevant reading. However, it may be that the area of interest is too specialised to find literature with an exact match. In this case, the search will need to be expanded. To make sure relevant literature is found, it is also important to think about alternative search words with a similar meaning, which authors of books and papers may have used instead of the chosen key words. For example, although they are distinct terms with their own definitions, 'learning disabilities' and 'learning difficulties' are often used interchangeably in the UK, but have significantly different meanings in the USA. Other terms (e.g. 'intellectual impairment') may also be used instead of 'learning disabilities'. In some cases both singular and plural versions of words will need to be searched. By ignoring these facts, time could be wasted with irrelevant reading or key information may be overlooked.

In looking for literature relating to 'From the Far Side', the key word 'transition' alone was far too broad, so additional key words needed to be added. If 'severe learning disabilities' was added, the range of literature found was too small, although it gave specific reading about the ability range of interest. However, if the word 'severe' was removed to leave 'learning disabilities', this gave access to a wider range of relevant literature, which generated more ideas and information. Experimenting with narrowing the search made the amount of literature found more manageable: using the key words 'transition' and 'learning disabilities' identified transitions at all ages in all circumstances, so adding the words 'adult', 'school' and 'young person' in different combinations reduced the recommended literature. This excluded some key texts, but it also brought other useful reading to the notice of the researcher. The reader may find it helpful to experiment with identifying the most useful research terms for their own main research question or practise using the research question for 'From the Far Side' above.

Connecting with libraries and other organisations

It is useful to contact a helpful librarian at the nearest local college or university with a department of education, and find out how to apply for a visitor's pass. Many university libraries allow some level of access to outside professionals, although they will probably ask for a letter of recommendation from an employer and other documentation as surety. In this way, practitioners may gain access to bound or electronic specialist journals which they would not otherwise be able to access.

The librarian should be able to advise practitioners on the most respected peer-reviewed journals in their area of inquiry, and show them how to search their own and other library databases for information relevant to their research question – both in book and article form. Recent Master's dissertations or PhD theses in the inquiry area can be very useful in terms of literature reviews, methods and analysis. The librarian may also be able to recommend charitable or other organisations related to an area of interest. These organisations can also offer advice and recommendations about key texts in their area. Some may have libraries of their own, and provide focused reading lists. Others may even be prepared to help with a specific literature search. In the absence of a local university library, a good local librarian may also be able to help.

Types of literature

Practitioners will commonly find a wide range of writing available on a chosen topic ranging from professionally published books, academic theses and journal articles written by specialists, through to writing in professional magazines, articles in the popular press, and online information from charitable organisations and special interest groups. Beware of heavily biased, unscientific, online promotional articles trying to sell products or training! It is important to start by reading books and articles of high quality. This means those written by authors who have established a good reputation in their field and published by publishers who have a proven track record in educational or related publishing.

Start by searching for the most recently published (usually within the past five to seven years), relevant articles in the most reputable scholarly or professional, peer-reviewed journals. These articles commonly begin with a brief overview of the literature supporting their topic, and end with a useful list of books they have used. If they are highly relevant to the inquiry topic, the articles are likely to reveal common references to foundational writing in the field. Foundational writing is the literature base that initiated important developments in a particular field. Practitioners should take note of these, and make them high priority on their reading list. It is important to use these foundational works to gain a firm understanding of their topic. In addition to reading the article, a scan of the reference list helps to discover other readings that have particular relevance for the inquiry topic. If a practitioner is lucky, there may be a recently published literature review which will give an instant overview in their areas of interest. These may be found as articles or booklets, or in Master's dissertations, PhD theses or government reports. Providing the review is of a sufficiently high standard, this can save precious time.

Another important area for any professional literature review is the government literature on policy and guidance, which has an impact on the inquiry topic. This can include not only the literature itself, but discussion papers on its interpretation.

A quick tip

When researching 'From the Far Side', the author found it useful to keep a running list of useful books and articles being read (see also 'References' section below). A traffic-light colour system to indicate priority was used – articles and books which were highly important to the topic were colour-coded green, those of medium interest were colour-coded orange, and those of minor interest but relevant were colour-coded red. After an article or book was read, the text of the reference was made bold so the completed readings could be easily tracked. There are other ways of prioritising reading, but it may help to keep some kind of 'at a glance' list of reading to date and intended future reading. It is also important to design a workable system which would help to organise what has been read and the notes taken (Lawson, 2007). Lawson makes the following suggestions for making sense of the information collected:

• Make sure it is relevant – read any summary descriptions of books and articles before starting to read to find out.
• Sort the information found into categories.
• Sort the information in these categories by how important it is.
• Keep notes on what is read – remember to include the full reference and the

page number, and to make clear whether the wording is the author's own or a summary (very important if you are to avoid plagiarism!).

Accessing the internet

The internet is a vast mass of shifting information. It is immensely valuable but with hazards on which unwary information seekers can run aground, and it helps to have a plan of how to access it. Harper and Houghton (2010) offer good advice. Much high quality material is tantalisingly out of reach, for example, academic journal articles are listed but are fully readable only by those with a university 'Athens' password or who are prepared to pay high sums to access articles online. However, if practitioners note down the full details of the articles they want to read, their local library may be able to request an article or chapter prints for a fee, although it will take several weeks to arrive. Other sites (e.g. online encyclopaedias) provide freely available information but without guarantee of accuracy. It *is* possible to find reputable information freely on the internet. For example, some respected authors make their papers available; charities publish research reports, information leaflets and guidance written by experienced specialists; government websites allow free download of most government literature. Some media sites have peer-created educational resource banks (e.g. the *Times Educational Supplement*) and provide access to other media (e.g. the Teachers' TV video archives). Again, having knowledge of reputable sources and writers will help to protect against misinformation.

Some researchers have preferences for specific internet search engines (e.g. Google, Google Scholar or Firefox). Google Scholar, for example, will identify scholarly writing only, which makes relevant reading easier to find, but may not pick up government or charitable literature.

Online databases

Practitioners can also use online databases to find writing in their inquiry area. If they are lucky enough to have access to a university library database through enrolment on a university course, it will be possible to search a range of subscription databases, and to access full text articles. However, there are also freely available databases (see below).

Databases provide high quality information, but in the largest ones, the quantity of information can be overwhelming! A librarian in a local or university library will be able to advise you, and, for a fee, libraries may be able to provide the articles and books you need through an interlibrary loans system.

Some useful free education databases include:

- *Educational Resources Information Center (ERIC):* a free digital library of education research and information (largely abstracts) dating back to 1966 (http://www.eric.ed.gov/);

- *the British Education Index (BEI)* – provides some free access, e.g. Education-line (http://www.leeds.ac.uk/bei/index.html);
- *the Institute of Education (UK)* databases including: IOE eprints http://eprints.ioe.ac.uk/ or Digital education resource archive http://dera.ioe.ac.uk/;
- CERUK (http://www.ceruk.ac.uk/) administered by the National Foundation for Educational Research.

What do I need to find out about?

The first step in beginning to read up on a chosen research question is to break it down into areas of reading. A search is unlikely to uncover information from other studies which relate exactly to the practitioner's area of interest. However, perhaps a previous study has focused on a similar topic but with a different group of children. It may be that the ideas which have been used in a different field could be adopted, or a combination of ideas from one or more studies could offer a meaningful background to an inquiry project (see Chapter 11). Naturally, if there is time, reading more widely is valuable and will bring in further ideas.

In reading for 'From the Far Side' (see research question above), there was no single body of writing that brought together all the aspects of interest, so a number of different topics within the broad area of learning disabilities (and variations) offered the background reading for the project. These were:

- interviews with professionals/families/students about transition;
- government policy and guidance about transition;
- how others had planned and managed post-school transition;
- other educational transitions (e.g. between early years settings and school or between junior and senior schools);
- overviews/discussions/debates of current issues around transition.

It may be helpful to take a research question and write down the different areas of reading which might be relevant to it.

Creating a reading list

Before starting to read, it helps to decide how to record the list of what has been read (i.e. a 'bibliography'). This needs to be an ongoing process, side by side with reading. Trying to track down information about books or papers that were read months ago is difficult, time-consuming and annoying. If *all* the relevant information about a book or paper is noted at the time of reading, finding it will take a matter of minutes. Putting this off is a big, time-intensive mistake!

Making a paper trail

Separate from this list, using the book details as a heading, it is important to take summary notes about the key points of what has been read. These may include details of memorable quotes (authors' exact words) – together with the page numbers on which they appear! – which can be used later to support the practitioner's own opinions. From a personal perspective, the author finds it useful to open a separate electronic file for every book or article she has read. She heads the page with the formal reference (see below) so that she has to hand all the information she needs without spending hours looking for it! She types each note on a separate line and numbers them with the relevant page(s) of the book or article she is reading, noting beside it whether what she has typed is a direct quote from the text, a summary of what the text said in her own words, or an idea of her own sparked off by something she read in the text.

How to reference

There are different styles that can be used for bibliographies and reference lists. If published books and journals are set side by side, it is easy to see that most lay out and punctuate the references very differently. However, in the individual book or publication, all the references are laid out according to a particular style. The important thing is that references are consistent and that all the information needed is there, so that readers who want to do so can trace the literature. In the text of articles and books, references use only author names and year dates in brackets. The full references appear as footnotes or at the end of the article. Table 3.1 sets out the information needed for full references.

The three most common kinds of literature to be referenced are illustrated in Table 3.1. Information from the internet can be referenced in a similar way, but must include the URL (webpage address) and the date on which it was accessed. The examples of the three most common types written in the form of a full reference below use the Harvard referencing system, where the date appears after the author names:

A journal article

Bondy, A. and Frost, L. (2001) 'The Picture Exchange communication system', *Behavior Modification*, 25(5): 725–744.

A book

Department of Health (2001) *Towards Person Centred Approaches: Planning with People*. London: DH Publications. [Online at: http://valuingpeople.gov.uk/dynamic/valuing people136.jsp; accessed: 25.5.10.]

Table 3.1 Information needed for references

Article	Book	Chapter in an edited book
Article author(s), family names and initials	*Book author(s), family names and initials*	*Chapter author(s), family names and initials*
The names of all authors should be noted. The author's name Edward P. Said would be noted as Said, E.P.		
Year of publication	*Year of publication*	*Year of publication*
This will be the same year as the date of the journal, magazine or newspaper	This will appear on the bibliographical information of the book, usually on the reverse of the book's title page or, occasionally, on the back cover	This is usually the year of the book's publication. Occasionally chapters are reprinted from earlier volumes or journals, in which case the date of publication is usually given on the first page of the chapter
Article title	*Title of book + any subtitle*	*Chapter title*
This is usually typed in normal type, and may be in quotation or speech marks	This is usually typed in italic, with the subtitle (if present) following the title separated by a colon	This is usually typed in normal type, and may be in quotation or speech marks
Journal title	*Place of publication*	*Book editor(s)*
This is usually written in italic, similar to a book title	This will appear on the imprint page of the book, usually on the reverse of the book's title page or, occasionally, on the back cover	Note the initials and family names of the editors. The word '(ed.)' for a single author and '(eds)' for more than one author should appear after the list of names
Volume number	*Publisher*	*Book title + any subtitle*
Most journals have a volume number which changes every year. In the absence of a volume number, use the date of publication (DD.MM) which usually appears on the front of the journal. (The year has already been noted.) This is sometimes in bold	This will be both on the cover and on the title page. The most detailed information is on the imprint page	This is usually typed in italic, with the subtitle (if present) following the title separated by a colon

Part number

Most journals are issued two or more times each year. If this is the case, they are given a part number corresponding to the part year. This can be displayed in brackets

Page numbers

It is important to note the page numbers of the article, so that the practitioner, or interested others, can locate it again

Place of publication

This will appear on the imprint page of the book, usually on the reverse of the book's title page or, occasionally, on the back cover

Publisher

This will be both on the cover and on the title page. The most detailed information is on the imprint page

Page numbers

It is important to note the page numbers of the chapter, so that the practitioner, or interested others can locate it again

A chapter in a book

Diniz, F.A. (1997) 'Working with families in a multiethnic European context', in B. Carpenter (ed.) *Families in Context: Emerging Trends in Family Support and Early Intervention*. London: David Fulton Publishers, pp. 107–120.

If needed, examples of reference styles for other kinds of literature (e.g. conference papers, personal correspondence, etc.) can be found in the reference sections of other articles or books.

Computer referencing software, often available with existing packages (e.g. Microsoft Office), allows a master list of reading to be kept. The above information can be entered into an ongoing electronic database. When short text references are included in the writing, the system will automatically compile a consistent list of references at the end of the paper.

To reference quotations, using the exact words that authors have written, the process is similar, except that the quotation usually stands alone, indented, with a line of white space above and below it, followed by the text reference in brackets, with the addition of the page number(s) from which it was taken.

The ethics of literature reviews

There is often much outrage when someone is wrongly quoted in the popular press. Accuracy is important when representing other people's words, and practitioners have a professional duty to make sure that accurate details of what authors actually wrote are kept. It is easy to misremember quotations, turning them into something that it is wished the author had said, rather than what the author actually did say. It is also essential that the spirit and intention of what the original author said are preserved, and that the quote is not used out of context to justify something completely different. Finally, whether a practitioner has summarised another's words and ideas or quoted them verbatim, it is vital that a full and accurate acknowledgement of the original source is made. To pass off someone else's words or ideas (even if reworded) in any other way is referred to as plagiarism. In its most serious form, plagiarism can lead to professional dismissal or prosecution under law.

Copyright law is another important consideration. When quoting or photo-copying others' published writing, there are legally binding limits on the proportion of the work that can be reproduced, even for educational purposes. Check with a local or university library for up-to-date restrictions. In most cases, a small number of words quoted in support of ideas and opinions for educational purposes and published work comes with an informal understanding between publishers and writers, known as 'fair dealing', whereby the person using a short quote is not expected to apply to the copyright holder for permission to use it. If in any doubt, take advice from a professional publishers' association or librarian. It is important to note that there is no such informal agreement in place for visual media, for which there is the added complication of gaining permission from the people appearing in them.

Finally, writing the review

A good literature review depends upon a closely defined research question. If a practitioner's inquiry is too wide, subsequent reading will be gappy, unfocused and unachievable. If it is too narrow, the reading will miss out on important ideas. Although as Lawson (2007) states, for a small-scale study you will need to read only a few texts, these need to be good quality texts, by reputable authors in the field, which help you to understand the key issues of your chosen area.

The review of literature is compiled based on the literature the practitioner has read and should underpin the inquiry about to be undertaken. It needs to start with an introduction to the inquiry, and a description of the key areas of the literature search relating to it. It should contain precise definitions of the key terms, preferably drawing on those of key authors. It then needs to review the key ideas and issues found in the literature relating to these areas, and the relevance these have to the inquiry the practitioner is about to undertake. The practitioner should end by giving the reasons why they are carrying out the research, and what they hope to discover that will increase their knowledge or improve their own, and maybe others', practice.

Carrying out a literature review allows the practitioner to place their research within the body of shared knowledge available to all practitioners, and ensure that their research is valuable. It helps them to find out what is already known about their area of interest, and understand its significance for their own practice. It also gives them access to other important perspectives. These will help to refine and shape the practitioner's own inquiry, perhaps leading to a change in the research question, setting it on firmer foundations and leading to more relevant outcomes for themselves and their students, so that their inquiry in turn will offer valuable insights for other practitioners and researchers to build on.

References

Aveyard, H. (2010) *Literature Review in Health and Social Care: A Practical Guide*, 2nd edn. Maidenhead: McGraw-Hill.

Harper, A. and Houghton, E. (2010) Tool-kit 10: using the internet to find educational research. *Practical Research for Education* 43: 6–13. [Online at: http://www.pre-online.co.uk/pre_toolkit.asp; accessed: 27.11.11.]

Hart, C. (1998) *Doing a Literature Review: Releasing the Social Science Research Imagination*. London: Sage.

Lawson, A. (2007) Tool-kit 5: what to do with the results of your literature search. *Practical Research for Education*, 38: 6–9. [Online at: http://www.pre-online.co.uk/pre_toolkit.asp; accessed: 26.11.11.]

McGill, P. (2010) Case study: a shared vision. In B. Carpenter, *A Vision for 21st Century Special Education*. London: Specialist Schools and Academies Trust (now The Schools Network).

Chapter 4

What are the possible ways to investigate what I want to know?

Understanding the family journey through a series of inquiry projects

Sally Conway and Teresa Whitehurst

Introduction

At this point in the ARC, the main questions for the inquiry have been established and there has been some exploration of what others have written on the subject. It is now time to consider how the inquiry should be framed. There are a variety of approaches to inquiry that frame a project and each has implications for the project. Making an informed decision about an approach that supports meaningful responses to the questions of inquiry is clearly important. All research and the resulting information it produces rest on three questions: (1) what is the nature of reality that underpins the research?; (2) what are the basic assumptions about the knowledge of reality that are being made?; and (3) how can the researcher find out about an area of inquiry? (Denzin and Lincoln, 2003). This chapter will focus on finding out about knowledge and framing in the context of an inquiry project.

When considering an inquiry project, there are three main types of approach or methodologies that can frame the process of inquiry: (1) quantitative; (2) qualitative; or (3) a mixed method design. A quantitative approach is often employed where statistics and numerical data are required and follows a very structured and fixed approach. This perspective seeks to obtain some representative objective, numerical measure of an object or phenomenon. Fixed designs are typically theory-driven and the phenomena of interest are typically quantified (Robson, 2002, p. 95). A qualitative design or flexible approach (ibid.) is employed to collect data related to people's experiences and perspectives of an issue. The qualitative perspective views the world as something to be understood through a dialogue of experience, understanding the way the world is from a particular viewpoint, while not discounting that other viewpoints may be equally valid; 'qualitative researchers study things in their natural settings, attempting to make sense of, or to interpret phenomena in terms of the meanings that people bring to them' (Denzin and Lincoln, 2003, p. 3). A mixed method approach is more eclectic and combines elements of each approach so that both qualitative and quantitative information can be collected to contribute to the overall result. This approach has emerged in recent years as a pragmatic solution to the so-called 'paradigm wars' between purist quantitative and qualitative researchers (Robson, 2002, p. 43).

To illustrate how different projects make use of different methodologies, this chapter discusses inquiry projects that were undertaken to explore the experiences of families who have a child with a label of autism spectrum disorder and complex needs at a residential special school in the United Kingdom. The chapter explains how families were engaged to achieve an understanding of their needs and to shape responsive service delivery. Working with parents as inquiry partners followed a 12-year journey, which enabled the family voice to become embedded within the development of the organisation. Sharing and understanding this journey will enable an appreciation of how a project of inquiry evolves and uses different methodologies to address different issues along the journey of research.

Context

The context for this long-term inquiry was a 52-week residential special school in the UK, offering care, education and therapies to children and young people with severe and complex learning needs, including autism, aged between 6 and 19. The school serves children and young people with the most complex learning difficulties and has an active Family Services department which considers the needs of the whole family including siblings, grandparents and significant others. In supporting families, it is important to recognise the significance of the mutual and reciprocal relationship between the family and the school. Parental involvement in children's education from an early age has a significant effect on educational achievement, and continues to do so into adolescence and adulthood (Sylva et al., 2004). While families often need support to be engaged in this process, they too can bring differing and essential viewpoints that enable a family service to be rooted in the holistic family perspective (Carpenter et al., 2005). The school discussed in this chapter places great emphasis on working closely with families to ensure that their voices are truly heard and inform service delivery.

The research journey

In order to develop a service that was responsive to family needs, the school embarked on a process of capturing family experiences, opinions and perspectives. Over a period of 12 years a variety of inquiry approaches were adopted to achieve a picture of how families perceived provision and what they wanted to see developed for the future. At the very beginning of the process, a mixed method inquiry design was adopted through a postal survey. The survey included closed and open-ended questions. This approach enabled the school to obtain a baseline of service delivery across the organisation and to measure the family response to prospective developments such as the introduction of a Family Services department. In order to analyse the impact of the action plan that emerged from the initial survey, a second survey was carried out two years later, which evaluated the introduction of the new initiatives that had emerged and highlighted opportunities for future development. A third survey was conducted a further two years later to again establish how far the organisation had moved to address family needs and ascertain any further areas for development. At this point it was evident that a mixed method approach using a survey, while initially useful in capturing the breadth of experience, was now no longer generating the depth of information necessary to move the school forward. It became apparent that specific areas of family service delivery needed further scrutiny using an alternative methodology. A move away from the mixed method approach, which collected a wide range of information but at a shallow level, to an approach that considered one issue in greater depth was considered to be more appropriate. Consequently, a qualitative approach was used to gain a richer family perspective of a specific area. The focus of this particular inquiry was the families' experiences of how they were supported and what it was like for them in moving their child to a residential school (Carpenter et al., 2005). To ensure the families felt their voices were truly being heard, a strong stakeholder focus was introduced. This was felt to be very important as often families have research done *unto* them rather than *with* them; 'the term "participant" suggests an active, willing engaging role rather than just a passive and possibly oblivious character' (Doyle, 2007, p. 85). A parent advisory group (PAG) was formed so that parents were central to the inquiry and guided how it was carried out. Incorporating this stakeholder focus then became a central component of how future inquiry projects were conducted.

After the more in-depth project had taken place, focused upon a specific issue, the school wanted to take another broad spectrum survey across all of the families. This involved returning to a mixed methodology approach as the families participating in the original three surveys had changed significantly. It was important to understand the perspective of the new families who had joined the school after the initial surveys. However, as the strong stakeholder focus approach adopted in the qualitative inquiry project had been so successful, the school decided to incorporate this aspect into the mixed methodology approach. This was achieved by including both the sibling and the parent perspective. This resulted in a Research Advisory Group (RAG) being formed that comprised both parents and sibling representatives. Outcomes from this group led the school to focus on a more in-depth area of inquiry to understand the specific needs of its sibling population with a focus on young adult siblings. The strong stakeholder focus was incorporated in the form of a sibling advisory group (SAG).

Employing differing approaches within the journey of inquiry

The following section enables practitioner researchers to understand why differing methodologies were used to frame specific projects, and more specifically how the advantages and disadvantages of these approaches influenced the development of the inquiry journey. This will enable the identification of elements of various approaches to be chosen to match the purpose of a particular study.

Mixed methods approach

Initially the school adopted a mixed methods approach in order to establish a baseline of families' perspectives of the current services available to them and to elicit their opinions of their anticipated future needs. As this was the first time families had been approached to share their thoughts, the mixed methods approach, using a survey with both open-ended and closed questions, was adopted in order to reach the whole population of families at the school. A mixed methods approach sees value in capturing both qualitative and quantitative information in the broadest sense, and as suggested by Robson (2002), can incorporate the following aspects:

- *Triangulation* – including three different processes to collect data.
- *Qualitative method used to facilitate fixed research design* – helps to provide information on context and participants.
- *Quantitative method used to facilitate flexible research design* – quantitative method (e.g. survey) used to help select participants in a flexible design.
- *Provision of a general or more complete picture* – quantitative method used to fill a gap in flexible design study (e.g. when the researcher cannot be present because of other research commitments); when the research questions raise issues which cannot be addressed by purely qualitative or purely quantitative methods.
- *Structure and process* – broadly speaking, fixed design research is more effective at getting at 'structural' aspects of social life, while flexible design research is more effective in dealing with processes. Combining them allows both aspects to be covered.
- *Researcher and participant perspectives* – fixed designs are typically focused on the researchers' perspective. Flexible designs can follow the participants' perspectives. A combined study can deal with both aspects.
- *Adding statistical generalisability* – flexible design research rarely permits statistical generalisability. Employing an additional qualitative and quantitative method may permit some generalisation.
- *Facilitating interpretation* – fixed designs are well adapted to establishing relationships between variables but are typically weak in establishing

the reason for them. Qualitative methods can help in developing explanations.

- *Relations between macro and micro levels* – qualitative methods tend to focus on the small-scale, micro, aspects of social life. Quantitative methods are often concerned with more large-scale, macro, aspects. Combining the two can help to integrate both levels.
- *Stage of the research* – different methods may be appropriate at different stages of the research process (for example, a fixed design study may be preceded by, or followed by, the use of qualitative methods).
- *Hybrids* – one way to combine the two approaches is to use qualitative methods in a fixed design or quantitative methods in a flexible design.

The first family project used a written survey posted to every family asking them to answer a series of generalised questions focusing on all aspects of service provision. This combined open (flexible) and closed (fixed) questions; open questions enable respondents to share experiences and perspectives in more depth, using a qualitative approach, while closed questions provide measurable objective data found in a quantitative approach. Information was therefore gathered using short tickbox-style questions, which could be counted to produce numerical information combined with the opportunity for families to expand their responses if they wished. As a tool, the survey provides the means to obtain a varied set of data from a wide population but has limitations on the depth of information that it gathers. In this instance the data provided the school with clear messages on a range of topics that affected families. For example, the survey used closed questions to probe the demographic profile of families, including distance the family travelled to visit their child and the number of people in the family, including the number of siblings. It also examined, via open questioning, opinions of current services available at the school such as education, care and therapies. The relevance of potential new services such as the introduction of a Family Service Department, Family Centres and information pertinent to family issues were explored to establish if these were needed and, if provided, the extent to which families would access them. Using a mixed methods approach enabled the school to gather a wide range of information which helped them to develop a targeted, informed action plan that was responsive to identified family needs.

Two years later, the school used the mixed methods approach again to measure the impact of the action plan formulated as a result of the initial baseline survey and to evaluate the introduction of the Family Services Department that families had identified as a requirement. While the question design was based upon the original survey, this was adapted to introduce a more qualitative approach to capture in-depth feedback from families about developments that had taken place since the last survey. This adaptation took the form of including more open-ended questions so families could contribute a broader range of perspectives. A two-year cycle of family inquiry had naturally emerged and so a further survey was conducted based on the previous two, again using a mixed methods approach, and once more including open questions to capture a broader range of families' perspectives. However, a pivotal point occurred once the data from the third survey were collated and analysed. It became evident that a mixed methods approach had ceased to generate the depth of information that the school was looking for in order to move forward in their family service provision. Additionally, it became apparent that much of the information the survey had generated was indeed repetitive. Therefore, a new approach was required to gain a deeper understanding of issues important to families.

Using a qualitative approach

The school needed to consider an alternative approach to its inquiry, which would enable an understanding of a richer family perspective. Having been aware for some time of the complexities around the initial placement of a child in a residential service, it was felt appropriate to consider the impact of induction and orientation for families. The induction process was defined as the period just before and just after the child joined the school and sought to consider how families felt at this time and what support was important to them. Due to the emotive nature of the subject a sensitive and more personal approach was required to support families to share their experiences of their own induction. While the mixed methods approach had provided a wide range of useful data to work with, it was clear that this project needed a qualitative stance that would enable deeper, richer data to emerge. The qualitative approach takes an interpretative perspective that Ritchie and Lewis (2003) have shown to be based on the following elements:

- directed at providing an in-depth and interpreted understanding of the social world of participants by learning about their social and material circumstances, their experiences, perspectives and histories;
- samples that are small in scale and purposively selected on the basis of salient criteria;
- data collection methods that usually involve close contact between the researcher and participants, which are interactive and developmental and allow for emergent issues to be explored;
- data that are very detailed, information-rich and extensive;
- analysis that is open to emergent concepts and ideas which may produce detailed description and classification, identify patterns of association, or develop typologies and explanations;
- outputs that tend to focus on the interpretation of social meaning through mapping and 're-presenting' the social world of the participants.

The school adopted these principles to underpin its inquiry. The Parent Advisory Group (PAG) kept the inquiry firmly rooted in the experiences of families who had already been through the induction process with their own child. The PAG met regularly to decide which approach to adopt and then to look at the issues that emerged. It was decided that the best way to obtain this in-depth and sensitive information was through a series of face-to-face semi-structured interviews conducted in the family home or a place of their choice. This decision was taken to create an environment where the family felt relaxed, in control, and able to share their thoughts. Although all families were invited to participate, only a small group were selected to share their experiences. This differs from the mixed methods survey approach that sought responses from all families. Selecting a smaller number of respondents was based on effectively managing the time-consuming process of gathering, transcribing and analysing a large amount of generated information from the interviews.

In addition to incorporating a strong stakeholder focus in the inquiry the school also wanted to involve more staff so that they would feel a sense of ownership of the process and outcomes which emerged. Having a level of ownership in an inquiry project encourages staff to be more likely to embed the outcomes in practice. This transdisciplinary element was central to the project and involved staff from across the breadth of the school including teachers, family workers, health professionals and care workers (Carpenter et al., 2007). The school was aware that staff and families represented on the PAG would need support to understand the process of inquiry so provided a one-day workshop covering the choice of methodology, how to conduct and manage qualitative interviews and to give them the skills to help build their confidence as new practitioner researchers.

A return to mixed methods

While the qualitative approach allowed the school to gain an in-depth perspective from a small number of families, time had lapsed since the last large-scale survey, during which time the family population had changed considerably. The newer families had not been given the opportunity to share their thoughts on the services offered by the school. Many of the services introduced as a result of the previous surveys had given this group of families a different starting point with service provision being much more established and offering a wider range of support mechanisms for families. This in turn meant that the new population had a much higher expectation of the school and it was important to gain a new perspective to work from in order to ensure that provision continued to develop in response to family need.

The mixed methods approach had proven useful in gaining a wide range of perspectives so it was felt this would be useful to repeat. However, lessons had been learnt along the way from the strong stakeholder focus, which had been incorporated into the qualitative approach. It seemed sensible therefore to blend this element into the mixed methods approach. The inquiry project therefore needed to consider how the PAG principle could be used within a survey approach. A Research Advisory Group (RAG) was formed which included both parent and sibling representatives. They helped to guide the planning and delivery of the survey to ensure it was again rooted in the family perspective. To ensure the inquiry was as inclusive as possible, an information day for families was arranged to gauge the most accessible method to conduct survey distribution, either via post, email or web access. The information day also offered families an opportunity to identify areas they felt were important to explore and the RAG then used this feedback to design the survey. Another change incorporated into the approach was to include a separate survey with fewer questions to capture the sibling perspective. The RAG considered the age range of the sibling population and designed two questionnaires to reflect the needs of older and younger siblings. This was a clear shift from previous surveys that had only asked for a generic family response which risked excluding the views and opinions of brothers and sisters.

Revisiting the qualitative approach

Realisation that the sibling perspective had been missing from previous inquiry projects led the school to explore this aspect further. A qualitative approach was felt to be the most appropriate, moving the inquiry approach away from the wider school population perspective back again to a narrower, more specific focus. As previous mixed methods approach had given a wealth of information on how to build and tailor support for the younger sibling population, the school decided to explore the experiences and needs of the young adult sibling population. Again the strong stakeholder focus was central to the approach and a Sibling Advisory Group (SAG) was developed to secure an accurate framework for this piece of work, setting it firmly in the context of the sibling experience.

The qualitative approach removed the boundaries that the mixed methods approach would have imposed and allowed siblings to explore their own perspectives in greater depth. It also provided an opportunity for engagement at a deeper level and encouraged siblings to share their experiences with confidence.

Conclusion

It is evident that the journey of inquiry this school embarked upon required an element of flexible thinking and a readiness to embrace change. As the outcomes of the inquiry allow new knowledge and new understanding to emerge, it is often the case that the type of approach to inquiry must also change. Being responsive and open to change enables the practitioner researcher to take an objective overview of their study path, identify new directions and respond to the challenges that this presents. Reflecting on a journey of inquiry allows an appreciation of what has influenced change and how understandings have also changed. Understanding an area of inquiry in the form of thoughtful questions to be explored, appreciating the way others have investigated this area and making decisions on how the inquiry can be explored will all help to decide upon the particular methodological approach to be adopted. Being open to changing this approach in response to inquiry outcomes is key to ensuring the knowledge continues to evolve, develop and deepen understanding. The inquiry journey explored in this chapter highlights that while there are merits in using a singular approach, the practitioner researcher should not feel rigorously bound by either a quantitative or qualitative approach but must consider the application of these approaches in relation to the purpose of the inquiry. In looking at previous projects there will be the opportunity to adopt a blended approach and identify successful elements of previous inquiries to enhance the design of an inquiry project. Ultimately, whether qualitative, quantitative or mixed methods are used, the importance lies in matching these approaches to the question posed and the type of information sought. Successfully matching these essential criteria will deliver outcomes that not only address the question posed but extend and add to the knowledge base for future practitioners.

References

Carpenter, B., Conway, S. and Whitehurst, T. (2005) First impressions. *Special Children*, July/August: 28–32.

Carpenter, B., Conway, S., Whitehurst, T. and Attfield, E. (2007) Journeys of enquiry: working with families in a research context. In B. Carpenter and J. Egerton (eds) *New Horizons in Special Education: Evidence Based Practice in Action*. Clent: Sunfield Publications.

Denzin, N. K. and Lincoln, Y. S. (eds) (2003) *Collecting and Interpreting Qualitative Materials*. 2nd edn. London: Sage.

Doyle, D. (2007) Transdisciplinary enquiry. In A. Campbell and S. Groundwater-Smith (eds) *An Ethical Approach to Practitioner Research*. Abingdon: Routledge.

Ritchie, J. and Lewis, J. (eds) (2003) *Qualitative Research Practice: A Guide for Social Science Students and Researchers*. London: Sage.

Robson, C. (2002) *Real World Research*. London: Blackwell Publishing.

Sylva, K., Melhuish, E., Sammons, P., Siraj-Blatchford, I. and Taggart, B. (2004) *Effective Pre-School Education. Final Report*. London: Institute of Education.

Chapter 5

Informed consent and assent

An ethical consideration when involving students in research

Ann Gillies

Introduction to informed consent

Navigating through the Accessible Research Cycle (ARC), practitioners have now successfully decided what they want to know and how they will apply it to their teaching. They have learned what others have had to say about their topic, and have thought about different ways to find out what they want to know; now it is time to ask a very important, complex question, "How does one involve people in research and obtain their informed consent?" This question is embedded within the ethical context of research considerations and obligations when working with participants. However, it also sits within a network of more general research ethics (American Educational Research Association, 2011; British Educational Research Association, 2011).

There is a specific systematic process to involving people ethically in research which includes obtaining informed consent. This is applicable to every participant in every research study, and can be especially complex when participants are children or vulnerable adults. Involving others in research must be done carefully to ensure participants understand what the research is about, how their involvement will be managed, and the possible benefits and risks, so they can make an informed decision about whether or not to take part. Students, families, and staff have rights they all need to be told about.

This chapter will introduce the reader to a logical sequence of actions to ensure ethical involvement of participants, and then tell a story of how one teacher worked through the process of obtaining informed consent and assent for the involvement of young children in a study in an inclusive elementary classroom. The reader will learn what the professional literature says about the ethical implications of facilitating informed consent and assent from students, and why this is such a critical step within the ARC.

After reading this chapter, readers will be more aware that the informed consent process sits within a network of ethical considerations. They will also be more aware of and sensitive to the complexities of ensuring children understand what they are being asked to do in research, that they have a choice, and a voice to clearly express whether or not to participate. The aim of this chapter is to motivate and prepare practitioners to follow meaningful informed consent processes for their projects, while taking into account important ethical considerations.

Research within the school context

When a school practitioner decides to engage in research with students, there are many ethical considerations regarding participants and research obligations. However, the first step, before ever students and parents are contacted, must be the approval of the research by the school, perhaps in liaison with a local university or college, to make sure it is ethically sound.

Ethics regarding involving participants include issues surrounding confidentiality, and the collection, sharing and storing of personal information. As a practitioner who works directly with students, one must be thoughtful about what constitutes knowledge outside the accepted teacher domain which should be kept confidential. There will be information gathered in practitioner research that cannot be shared with others, including private opinions and private information. Practitioners are faced with the ethical dilemma of determining which information to keep confidential and which information can be shared to support education.

Data protection is also an important ethical consideration for the security of the participants and the fidelity of the research. The practitioner has an obligation to collect only data which is needed for the current research, and also to store the information securely, safe from breaches of confidentiality and harm to materials. When a practitioner shares information and outcomes from the research with participants and families, it must be done in an appropriate way, ensuring anonymity. An added complication is whether, in an environment where a student is known well, even anonymous information could be recognized as relating to a particular student or their family. If this is the case, it is important to be open with parents and students about the level of confidentiality which can be achieved.

Briefly taking a wider ethical perspective, there are also many other issues a practitioner should also think through, including whether their research is principled and relevant, how to make sure that their evidence is useful and useable by choosing appropriate ways of collecting and interpreting evidence, the need to take account of other research in their area, and to share outcomes from their own research so that others can evaluate it, learn from it and repeat it. Practitioners may come under pressure from colleagues or funders to ignore unwelcome findings, or change outcomes. These must be resisted – if necessary with support from a trusted colleague. Schools which have strong and supportive research structures will cover all these issues in their own research policy and ethical code.

Approaching participants

Once school approval has been obtained for the research project, and participants are identified and recruited for an inquiry project, the researcher must obtain informed consent from students' parents or guardians and then the students themselves before involving students in actual research. Practitioners need to follow a process that ensures to the maximum level possible that there is informed consent. When a research study includes student participants, informed consent must be given by parents or guardians, and assent must be given by the student participants. (Asking for consent from a minor is referred to as assent.) These are two separate processes, with consent from parents/guardians needing to be addressed first.

Informed consent and assent mean that parents/guardians and students have agreed to involvement in the inquiry after all information about the study and their own rights have been shared with them at a level which is completely understandable to them. This means that, in addition to realizing their rights, everyone involved knows what the study is about, how it will be done, what the student's role is within the study, and what benefits or risks will ensue from the participation of the student (Ross, Sundberg, & Flint, 1999). In some cases, parents of student participants may have difficulties with literacy, so researchers may need to explore communicating vital information in ways apart from written means.

It is critical to inform and explain research participants' rights in a way that is age- and ability-appropriate so that the consent/assent given by parents and students is built on meaningful understanding of the research. According to Yeager-Woodhouse and Sivell (2006), practitioner researchers have a moral and ethical responsibility to do the following:

- ensure participants' confidentiality;
- consider the possible consequences from participation in their study;
- clearly explain what participation means;
- present the opportunity to participate or not to participate in a non-threatening, non-coercive way;
- offer the option to withdraw without penalty at any point in the study.

Listening to and respecting the answers received from students and parents is also important. Practitioner researchers are then challenged to facilitate appropriate ways for students to deliver the clear message "Yes, I want to participate" or "No, I don't want to." The process of informing students about a research project, asking for their assent in an appropriate manner, and then being able to accurately receive the message of acceptance or denial will likely be unique for each student, especially if a practitioner works with students who may have disabilities.

The project

A teacher who included her students with autism in a general education Kindergarten class agreed to collaborate with a professor on a project aimed at eliciting student views on ideas about inclusion. This project occurred in a middle-sized public elementary school in southwest Florida in the United States.

The challenge

As the teacher made her way through the ARC Stage Four, "How am I going to involve people in my research and enable their informed choice?" became a challenging question. Not only did the teacher have to think about obtaining approval from the county school district, the building principal, and the Kindergarten classroom teacher, she had to consider the best way to obtain informed consent from parents and guardians, and then assent from each and every student in the inclusive classroom. As the teacher was completing steps to begin her research with students, she had to expand her thinking about the ethical considerations involved in each step of the process with participants and in the research process.

The students were aged 5 or 6 years old and were all different in terms of their ability levels, communication styles, and life experiences. It was critical for all students to have the opportunity to participate in the research project and have their voices heard, but going through the informed consent process became very complex with many ethical considerations.

The informed consent process

Through the process to obtain informed consent from each of her students, the teacher realized how individualized and differentiated this process needs to be. In this chapter, one way to approach this critical stage in the ARC will be presented, with the acknowledgement that there are many other ways. Each practitioner researcher will have to modify and adapt the informed consent/assent process for each of his or her student participants to ensure the process matches the different ways students, especially students with disabilities, communicate.

Step one

The first step of the informed consent process in this research project was explaining the study, in great detail, to the school building principal and Kindergarten teacher. This was done after school in a face-to-face meeting with the three professionals. Ethically, research needs to be shared and discussed with stakeholders and staff in charge of students to ensure student safety and security. The teacher presented all of the information about the project, the project aims and outcomes, and answered questions from both the principal and Kindergarten teacher. The adults agreed students would not be harmed from participation in this research. With their understanding and approval, the teacher continued on with the process.

Step two

The next step was the submission of a formal Institutional Review Board (IRB) research application to the county school district obtained from the school district website. The UK equivalent would be an application to a research and ethics committee – either school- or university-based. To complete the IRB application, the teacher developed a written letter intended for parents and guardians informing them about the research study, outlining their rights, and explaining the rights of the children. Due to the active involvement of the university professor who developed the booklet in this research study, it was also necessary to submit another formal IRB research application to the university in which she worked.

Step three

Once IRB formal and written approval had been received from both institutions, the teacher researcher explained the study to parents and guardians through emails, written correspondence, over the telephone, and/or in person, letting them know that a formal consent form would soon be sent home with their children. An ethical consideration for practitioners to address is how to best inform parents of their rights in relation to research projects. Student and parent rights are oftentimes written into the formal consent form as was the case in this project. Figure 5.1 illustrates the first written correspondence sent home to parents informing them of the project, an informal note about the study.

A copy of the children's booklet used in the study was sent home with the informed consent information for parents to review. They were also encouraged to ask questions and give feedback about the booklet and the project to the teacher. The formal IRB-approved letter of consent was then sent home for parents to sign. Figure 5.2 illustrates the formal written correspondence sent home to parents asking for their signature to indicate their informed consent of their son/daughter participating in the project.

Once all letters of informed consent were signed and returned, the teacher began the process of informing students about the project.

Step four – enabling informed consent/assent for all

An important step in obtaining informed consent for minors always involves the parents or guardians. Any research study involving students must be reviewed by an Institutional Review Board (IRB) which ensures the students' rights of confidentiality and freedom from harm are protected, and the IRB requires parental letters about the research to be signed for their informed consent (Gall, Gall, &

Children's Views of Inclusion Project

Dear Parents and Family Members,

I am involved in a project with my professor from the University of South Florida about listening to what children have to say about being included, having fun, joining in, and learning together. All of these things have to do with inclusion, which is the joining together of students who are typically developing and students with disabilities. Your child has been a part of an inclusion class since the beginning of the school year and I think has engaged in a wonderfully successful experience benefitting not only the students with disabilities, but every child. The project I am doing involves inviting your child to share a booklet with me that has pictures of them having fun, joining in, and learning together, and then having a conversation about these pictures. I have taken pictures of the students and wish to use 3 of them for the booklet with your permission. These pictures will be used in my interviews with the whole class and might be published in a chapter of a book entitled *Confronting Obstacles to Inclusion*. The chapter I am assisting with is "Engaging Young Children in Research about an Inclusion Project." Your child's name will not be on the individual booklets, or appear anywhere in the book.

I am asking your permission to include a photograph with your child in a booklet to be used at ######## and then possibly published in *Confronting Obstacles to Inclusion*. Please sign below to indicate your permission and contact me with any questions. You are welcome to stop by the classroom to see the photographs at your convenience. Thank you.

I grant permission for a photograph of my child _____
to be used in a project at ######### Elementary and to possibly be published in *Confronting Obstacles to Inclusion*.

_____   _____
Signature
                                        Date

Please contact me with any questions:
Ann Gillies

Figure 5.1 Informal information and photo consent form

Borg, 2007). For this project, the teacher learned that she needed to use different communication modes to reach all of the parents and guardians of the 23 students involved in her research project. Many parents dropped their children off and picked them up from school daily, so that enabled face-to-face contact. Other parents worked full-time, and the telephone or email was more convenient for them. Two families did not have telephones or computers, so notes were written and transported back and forth between school and home via the students' backpacks. The teacher contacted every parent prior to sending the written informed consent document home to be signed to informally introduce the study to ensure family members understood exactly what was being asked of their children.

The teacher began the assent process with the students first as a group, then individually, and then asking them, one at a time at their own level, if they

IRB Approval
FWA 90001609

IRB Number: 107433I

From   2-3-09

Thru   2-2-10

January, 2009

Dear Parents,

As a USF graduate student, I am currently working on a research project with my professor entitled "Children's Views of Inclusion". I am writing to ask if you would be willing to consider your son/daughter participating in this project, which is about the inclusion of students with disabilities in our classroom. This project aims to gather perspectives of children around established key concepts related to inclusion like belonging, working together, and having fun together. This project is intended to inform the understandings and practices of teaching students with and without disabilities together effectively.

Dr. Phyllis Jones, a University of South Florida professor in the College of Education, is the developer of this project and our wishes are to invite each child to share a picture booklet entitled *Being Included* with me that focuses on inclusion, and then have a conversation about it. I would record your child's verbal responses to given prompts about the pictures in the booklet. This approach to data collection has been used successfully to gather views of children. The sharing of the booklet will not take longer than 15–20 minutes and would be done during a non-academic instructional time during the school day. Children's names will not be placed on the booklets to ensure their responses remain anonymous. Dr. Jones and I will manage and analyze the data and write articles/book chapters for dissemination. We may also present at professional conferences. The booklets will be held in a secure location for up to three years after the completion of the project. However, certain people may need to see your child's study records. By law, anyone who looks at your child's records must keep them completely confidential. The only people who will be allowed to see these records are:

• Certain government and university people who need to know more about the study. For example, individuals who provide oversight on this study may need to look at your child's records. These include the University of South Florida Institutional Review Board (IRB) and the staff that work for the IRB. Individuals who work for USF that provide other kinds of oversight to research studies may also need to look at your child's records.

• Other individuals who may look at your child's records include: agencies of the federal, state, or local government that regulates this research. This includes the Department of Health and Human Services (DHHS) and the Office for Human Research Protections. They also need to make sure that we are protecting your child's rights and safety.

If you have questions about your child's rights, general questions, complaints, or issues as a person taking part in this study, call the Division of Research Integrity and Compliance of the University of South Florida at (813) 974-9343.

We would appreciate your support in this project and believe that a conversation between you and your child about sharing the booklet with me will positively contribute to the

Figure 5.2 IRB approved consent form

wanted to participate. Information about the study, at an appropriate level for 5–6-year-olds and for students with differing learning, language, and cognitive abilities, was presented to the Kindergarten class in a variety of formats:

- The booklet was first shown to the class as a whole; each of the pictures was shared and sample questions were read aloud.
- The teacher researcher described the purpose of her inquiry as follows: "I would like to talk with each of you to learn how you feel about being with others at school. We can look at these pictures together and talk about them."
- To protect the students' right of deciding whether or not to participate in the study, the teacher researcher invited each student individually to share the booklet versus assuming their participation; "Would you like a turn to look at the pictures and talk with me?"
- Some students were enthusiastic to begin the booklet immediately when asked, and some students wanted to talk more about what was expected of them.
- Two of the students with labels of autism along with several other of the classmates who were easily distracted and sometimes overstimulated were led away from the busy work area in the classroom, one at a time, and asked if they wanted to participate in the booklet in a quieter, less distracting part of the room.

The teacher took her time asking for assent from each and every student, moving at each student's own pace. This multi-dimensional approach was successful in ensuring students were better able to process and understand the verbal invitation to participate with the booklet and have time to think, decide, and formulate a response to the invitation with minimal distractions. The students were all able to verbally give their clear assent to participate.

Several of the general education Kindergarteners had language difficulties or were learning English as a second language, so the teacher brought the picture booklet to them individually, pointed to the booklet, pointed to the toy area where she had shared the booklet with other students, and asked "Want turn?" If the student followed the teacher with an enthusiastic, happy facial expression, said "Yes" or "Si," and sat down excited to look at the picture booklet, then the teacher interpreted those words and behaviors as assent to participate. If a student seemed hesitant about following the teacher, looked worried or anxious, said "No" or shook his or her head, then the teacher would have interpreted those behaviors as a student's message of not wanting to share the booklet and would have accepted that student's right to refuse participation.

Another example of how the teacher's observations and interpretation of student behavior supported informed consent/assent was with one of the students with autism as well as another student with the label of gifted. These two students were very interested in what the teacher was doing with the booklet and had a lot of questions. The teacher understood this repeated question-asking as something her student with autism did when feeling unsure about doing something different or new, so she took a great deal of time to answer each question the student asked repeatedly until he felt secure in giving an answer of "Yes, it's my turn" and moving to the toy area where the booklet was. The other student was interested in more in-depth explanations about the purpose of the project, what the questions were about, and why there were no "right" answers to any of the questions. The teacher thought this student may have similar unsure feelings of engaging in something out of the normal class routine, so she took extra time to answer that student's questions as well. Both of these students used a lot of verbal explanation to give their assent to participate.

Another student with autism, who is an emerging communicator and who benefits from specialized behavior support, was offered an opportunity to participate in this study within a structured work area in his self-contained classroom. This was a setting where he was accustomed to working with the teacher. The work area was highly visual, had a familiar and predictable work routine, and was equipped with his individualized communication supports. These supports were picture symbols of "help," "break," "all done," numerals 1–3 to indicate work tasks, and a card with illustrations of the four feelings "happy," "sad," "angry," and "scared." The practitioner put the picture booklet into a work bin within the work system, and from observation of the student's happy facial expressions, calm and regulated body language, use of familiar picture symbols, and enthusiastic engagement in the booklet, she interpreted the student's behavior as a message to mean assent to participate. Figure 5.3 illustrates the card used with illustrations of the four feelings "happy," "sad," "angry," and "scared."

Emerging issues

By treating each student in this diverse inclusive classroom as a unique individual and recognizing the specialized supports needed to enable understanding of

Figure 5.3 Visual support for assent

what was being asked of him or her, the teacher was able to invite each student to participate in the research study and felt confident that assent was granted in an appropriate and ethical way, at each child's own level, from all of the student participants. The assent process looked different for each student and a variety of accommodations and modifications were used, including movement to a less stimulating context, extended time for students to decide, gesture prompts, extra verbal explanations, modified verbal explanations, extended time to look at the pictures, extra time to ask questions, a structured and highly visual work area, and the use of picture symbols. The informed consent stage of this project took the teacher a great deal of time over a six-week period to complete, but because the accommodations and modifications had been made, every member of the inclusive class had an opportunity to independently voice his and her acceptance or refusal to participate in the study.

The teacher's use of observations and interpretation of student behavior in this critical informed consent/assent stage of the study was problematic and also very positive; without these strategies, important voices would be missing.

Ethical implications of informed consent

The importance of involving students in research projects, the significance of conducting research "with" children as opposed to "on" children, and the ethical responsibility for enabling children's informed choice are being better realized in the literature (Brainard, 2003; Norwich & Kelly, 2004). The inclusion of the voices of students with disabilities in research, students with severe and complex disabilities, and especially students with communication issues, demands even more attention. This group of students is consistently marginalized and missing from the literature in education (Jones, 2005; Snelgrove, 2005) and practicing researchers need to follow an ethical framework to obtain informed consent from students with intellectual and communication challenges. This is very challenging and has rarely been done in educational research, but this does not mean it should not be done. Practitioner researchers need to be creative, student-centered, and find ways to support student participation in this critical stage of the ARC with every participant. Coupled with the need to involve more students in research is the need to carefully examine the individualized process required to obtain informed consent and assent from students with diverse learning needs.

Statistics have estimated that half of the U.S. population reads at or below an 8th grade level, and despite this statistic most consent forms are written at about the 11th grade level (Brainard, 2003). A practitioner researcher must follow best practices for parental participation to support informed consent in his or her research project. Best practices to consider when involving parents are:

• ensuring consent forms are at a readable level for parents and guardians;
• ensuring consent forms are in parents'/guardians' primary language;

- directly involving parents in the consent process to facilitate a better understanding of their rights and the rights of their children as participants.

Ways to increase parental participation in the informed consent process include:

- organize a parent orientation meeting where consent forms are handed directly to parents (Stein, Jaycox, Langley, Kataoka, Wilkins, & Wong, 2007);
- supplement informed consent forms with videotapes or CD-ROMs (Brainard, 2003);
- use multiple, culturally appropriate communication channels (principal's newsletter, PTA meetings, telephone trees), translating when needed (Ross et al., 1999);
- consider appropriate communication methods based on class; for example, it is not appropriate to assume every family has a computer in their home (Frye, Baxter, Thompson, & Guinn, 2002).

After informed consent has been obtained from parents or guardians, there are ethical considerations needed when working through the assent process in schools with students (Norwich & Kelly, 2004). Practitioner researchers may need to give attention to the way in which students are asked. Ethical dilemmas include asking for assent at the level of the student, supporting student understanding of the project, ensuring a student's ability to refuse to participate in the research study, pressure on a student from a practitioner to participate, and a student's right to receive the best educational instruction. A suggestion offered by Bournot-Trites and Belanger (2005) to support practitioner researchers is to have a third party, who advocates for the students, oversee and/or manage the consent/assent process. With outside involvement from a party with a vested interest in the welfare of the students, a practitioner will have extra support in ensuring ethical dilemmas are addressed and students are protected. Figure 5.4 illustrates the steps in the process to obtain informed consent for students to participate in a research project.

Individualization of the informed consent/assent process is often necessary and it is essential that strategies adopted to obtain assent should align with the student's cognitive, language, and communication abilities. Additional attention may need to be paid to enable a student with a disability to choose whether or not to participate in a research study. This needs to be done in a way to respect and value his or her personal autonomy and dignity (Guess, Benson, & Siegel-Causey, 2008; Mactavish, Mahon, & Lutfiyya, 2000). For example, the student with autism in this project benefitted from being asked to share the booklet when it was presented to him in his familiar work area. He had learned throughout the school year that his structured work area was a place where he interacted with

1. Explain project to school staff (principal, involved teachers, etc.) and get their approval.
2. Develop an informed consent letter for parents/guardians that clearly explains the project and outlines students' rights.
3. Complete an Institutional Review Board (IRB) application from the school district and get their formal approval.
4. Inform parents/guardians of the project in detail and in an appropriate way for each family; when they understand the project and their rights, ask them to sign the IRB-approved informed consent letter.
5. Inform children of the project in detail and in an appropriate way for each of them individually; when they understand the project and their rights, ask them whether or not they want to participate in the project.
6. Constantly monitor children throughout the duration of the project and remind them of their right to withdraw at any time.

Figure 5.4 Steps to obtain informed consent when involving children in research

teachers and gave responses to work tasks that were placed in the work system. The practitioner felt that if she presented the booklet to him in this familiar context, the student would better understand the teacher was expecting a response from him regarding whether or not he wanted to engage in the task. Based upon knowledge gained about this student from observations of his behavior in the past, the teacher was able to interpret the student's behavior within the work area and understand his responses using picture symbols as meaning "Yes, I would like to participate."

Recognition of nonverbal signals for students who are emerging communicators and being responsive to those signals is an appropriate way a practitioner can invite students with complex disabilities to participate in research (Guess et al., 2008). Knowing and responding appropriately to signals from students illustrate the importance of the practitioner–student relationship.

Inherent in research done by practitioners are ethical issues in the already existing practitioner–student relationship. One ethical dilemma is a practitioner's dual-role conflict between the demands of teaching and the demands of his or her research (Hammack, 1997). A practitioner researcher must be aware of time constraints in fulfilling obligations for both roles, the effects of his or her power over students, and of maintaining a fair and ethical commitment to both roles as practitioner and researcher.

Lewis and Porter (2008) emphasize the importance of practitioners' ethical obligation to recognize their students' rights, and offer practitioner researchers a set of guidelines for self-evaluation that can be used throughout all stages of the ARC. The guidelines present questions regarding research aims and ethics, sampling, design, and communication. Two examples of questions a practitioner should ask him or herself during the informed consent stage are: Is consent/ assent confirmed throughout the research?, and, Have participants, at appropriate intervals, been reminded of their right to withdraw? (Lewis & Porter,

2008, p. 7). This self-evaluation calls for ongoing informed consent/assent rather than a one-time step in the research project.

Practitioner researchers must ensure student and family confidentiality is maintained throughout the study, being careful not to disclose any pertinent information to other staff members in the teacher's lounge, staffroom, or other informal places where his or her role as a teacher may allow such discussion. This possible dual-role conflict demands careful and ongoing attention for the protection of the student participants.

Conclusion

School personnel, researchers, and practitioners acknowledge the heterogeneity of students in today's classrooms, which emphasizes the need to act thoughtfully and responsibly to student differences (Sapon-Shevin, 2003). Responding ethically to Stage Four of the ARC, involving the informed consent and assent from all students, is done through this thoughtful and responsible attention to student differences.

Presented in this chapter was an example of how one teacher researcher faced the challenge of involving 23 children in research and obtaining informed consent and assent from this group of very different students. This practitioner researcher learned how to invite students with differing cognitive, language, and learning abilities to participate in research in a way that was understandable, comfortable, and meaningful to each of them. She did this by differentiating the way in which children were invited to participate (Ross et al., 1999). It illustrated that the greater shared understanding about the research led to the children making more informed choices about whether or not to participate (Yeager-Woodhouse & Sivell, 2006).

Being aware of and accepting of student differences, and adapting and modifying the informed consent process, were being responsive to the children's differences. Working through the informed consent/assent process individually with each student gave every member of the class a voice that was respected and valued and that added to the knowledge base about inclusive school experiences.

Practitioners must work harder and more creatively to seek assent from all children and aim to achieve higher levels of certainty that the responses children are giving are really assent. Practitioners are responsible for understanding and respecting who their student participants are and keeping each child and family safe from all harm. As practitioners struggle with legislation's call for more evidence-based practice and acknowledge the research to practice gap that exists in education, the ARC introduces a way to bridge this gap and guide practitioners to conduct their own meaningful research projects in applied settings with student participants. This chapter has shone a light on the Fourth Stage, involving students in research and obtaining informed consent, and has highlighted the complex yet worthwhile process that can be tailored for each unique student participant. This has been done in the context of a literature base that reiterates the importance of offering all students the chance to participate in research in an ethical and dignified way.

References

American Educational Research Association (2011). *Code of ethics.* Washington, DC: AERA. [Online at: http://www.aera.net/uploadedFiles/About_AERA/Ethical_Standards/CodeOfEthics(1).pdf; accessed: 27.11.11.]

Bournot-Trites, M., & Belanger, J. (2005). Ethical dilemmas facing action researchers. *Journal of Educational Thought, 39*(2), 197–215.

Brainard, J. (2003). Study finds research consent forms difficult to comprehend. *The Chronicle of Higher Education, 49*(19), 21–22.

British Educational Research Association (2011). *Ethical guidelines for educational research.* London: BERA. [Online at: http://www.bera.ac.uk/files/2011/08/BERA-Ethical-Guidelines-2011.pdf; accessed: 27.11.11.]

Frye, F., Baxter, S., Thompson, W., & Guinn, C. (2002). Influence of school, class, ethnicity, and gender on agreement of fourth graders to participate in a nutrition study. *Journal of School Health, 72*(3), 115–120.

Gall, M.D., Gall, J.P., & Borg, W.R. (2007). *Educational research: An introduction.* Boston, MA: Pearson.

Guess, D., Benson, H.A., & Siegel-Causey, E. (2008). Concepts and issues related to choice making and autonomy among persons with severe disabilities. *Research & Practice for Persons with Severe Disabilities, 33*(1–2), 75–81.

Hammack, F. (1997). Ethical issues in teacher research. *Teachers College Record, 99,* 247–265.

Jones, P. (2005). Inclusion: lessons from the children. *British Journal of Special Education, 32*(2), 60–66.

Lewis, A., & Porter, J. (2008). Interviewing children and young people with learning disabilities: Guidelines for researchers and multi-professional practice. *British Journal of Learning Disabilities, 32*(4), 191–197.

Mactavish, J.B., Mahon, M.J., & Lutfiyya, Z.M. (2000). "I can speak for myself": Involving individuals with intellectual disabilities as research participants. *Mental Retardation, 38*(3), 216–227.

Norwich, B., & Kelly, N. (2004). Pupils' views on inclusion: Moderate learning difficulties and bullying in mainstream and special schools. *British Educational Research Journal, 30*(1), 43–65.

Ross, J., Sundberg, E., & Flint, K. (1999). Informed consent in school health research: Why, how, and making it easy. *The Journal of School Health, 69*(5), 171–176.

Sapon-Shevin, M. (2003). Inclusion: A matter of social justice. *Educational Leadership, October,* 25–28.

Snelgrove, S. (2005). Bad, mad and sad: Developing a methodology of inclusion and a pedagogy for researching students with intellectual disabilities. *International Journal of Inclusive Education, 9*(3), 313–329.

Stein, B., Jaycox, L., Langley, A., Kataoka, S., Wilkins, W., & Wong, M. (2007). Active parental consent for a school-based community violence screening: Comparing distribution methods. *Journal of School Health, 77*(3), 116–120.

Yeager-Woodhouse, D., & Sivell, J. (2006). Prepackaged tour versus personal journey: The meaning of informed consent in the context of the teacher-study group. *Journal of Academic Ethics, 4*, 189–203.

Chapter 6

Voice for Choice

Victoria Hobday

Introduction

There are many and varied ways to collect information and to use it within a school-based project. This chapter illustrates how a range of different methods can be used in the data collection process and considers how these were made accessible to young people. The idea of the Voice for Choice project arose out of the need to support children with severe learning disabilities and limited communication methods to have more control over their lives, particularly with regard to the therapies in which they were involved and medical regimes to which they were often subjected. While it is well acknowledged that medical regimes and therapeutic interventions are key to a young person's well-being, the extent to which they are consulted and involved in these decisions is limited, particularly when the child has a learning disability and finds it difficult to communicate. The project sought literally to give these young people a 'voice' to make choices through different communication strategies and to ensure the process was inclusive and participatory by listening directly to the voices of those involved. This chapter will help practitioner researchers to understand the various ways of collecting information, how to explore the strengths and weaknesses of each one and how to ensure that the information gathered is fit for the purpose. It will also enable the practitioner researcher to understand the importance of adapting data collection tools to suit the people involved in the project.

The Voice for Choice project was conducted at a 52-week residential school for children with severe and complex learning needs in the United Kingdom with around 70 per cent of the population being diagnosed as having autistic spectrum disorder (ASD). The school is set in a rural community and comprises of ten bungalows, each housing approximately six students. The students primarily live at the school all year round, returning home for visits at weekends and holidays. Families are also encouraged to visit the students frequently, with accommodation provided on site. Student education takes place in a purpose-built school with students being taught in class groups of five or six students supported by a teacher and a number of teaching assistants. Due to the complex needs of the students, the staff ratio both in the school and in the residential home is normally on a 1:1 basis but occasionally students require 2:1 support.

The project began with the premise that that young people with learning disabilities are likely to have less choice and control over factors which affect their lives. Clarke, Olympia, Jensen, Heathfield and Jensen (2003) proposed that the risk of children with ASD or learning disabilities developing psychiatric disorders and other mental health problems may increase as a result of little control over their lives, with learned helplessness being a particular factor associated with the onset of depression, negative self-esteem and negative self-concept. The need for schools to promote and sustain emotional well-being and positive mental health in young people with learning disabilities is crucial (Foundation for People with Learning Disabilities, 2001) but ways in which opinions of individuals with limited verbal communication can be meaningfully elicited are limited (Porter, 2003).

To increase involvement of young people with learning disabilities to make choices about the therapies they received, the Voice for Choice Project designed a variety of resources to promote communication and trialled these with young people and practitioners. These resources included:

- *Student-focused information booklets*. These booklets were designed to enable students to make choices by giving them information. Each booklet varied according to a particular therapy but gave the student information about the people who would be involved in their therapy, what they could expect to happen at the therapeutic session and where this would take place. The information was supported by the individual's unique method of communication either in photos, symbols or words.
- *Communication cards*. This was designed as a passport-style card for students to take to medical appointments. The card contained brief information on how the student preferred to communicate, and other key pieces of information that could be beneficial to enhance communication and meaningful interactions during the appointment.
- *Behaviour Development Plans (BDPs)*. These plans are created for all students living at the provision to support and promote positive behaviour. Historically, BDPs had been designed by a multi-disciplinary team but without the benefit of student involvement. The Voice for Choice project reviewed the BDPs and trialled BDP a more inclusive document, enabling the student to have greater input into goal setting and evaluation.
- *Physical interventions' booklet*. 'Holding You and Keeping You Safe' was a booklet created to increase the student's understanding of why physical interventions were necessary to help to keep them and others safe. By understanding the need for physical interventions it was anticipated that there would be a reduction in the student's level of anxiety at the time of the intervention and that a mechanism for discussing their feelings about

the incident could be incorporated to try to reduce associated anxiety and promote debriefing with students following incidents.

- *Choice boards*. General daily choices that were routinely offered to students were enhanced through the use of choice boards. These were introduced to increase the frequency of choices offered and to develop choice-making skills in order to give students greater confidence, skills and practice in their choice-making activities. Higher-level decision-making such as that involved in individual treatments and therapeutic interventions relies on an individual being confident in making everyday choices decisions.

The Voice for Choice project focused on developing, trialling and modifying these resources, gathering evidence and testing out their effectiveness, strengths and limitations.

By the end of the chapter a practitioner researcher will be able to do the following:

- be able to consider various approaches to collecting information and understand each method's strengths and weaknesses;
- understand the factors which will impact on the quality of the data;
- appreciate that the methods used to gather the information will need to be appropriate to the type of project being undertaken and the type of questions which are being asked;
- understand how to adapt the ways in which information might be gathered to be meaningful to students with emerging communication skills;
- understand how the use of a variety of approaches looking at the same issue can strengthen the outcomes of the project and make findings more reliable.

Gathering information

The Voice for Choice project was conducted within a multi-disciplinary environment where students were often supported on a 1:1 basis. This meant that the project could gather a wealth of information from practitioners working closely with the young people on a daily basis. This diverse, multi-disciplinary team included teaching staff, care support staff, speech and language therapists, occupational therapists, psychologists, play therapists, and music therapists in addition to information from parents and guardians. Collecting information from all of these different individuals provided a very rich account of the young people which helped to shape the type of resources which would be most appropriate to develop choice making skills. Using a mixed methods design meant the project was able to use a variety of approaches to find out information; including questionnaires, observations and interviews.

Who was involved?

The project involved seven students between the ages of 10 and 16. Five students were male and two were female. It was important for the project that each student had a diagnosis of having a learning disability, and a mental health condition, and was experiencing difficulties with communication as this was the population for whom the resources were being developed. Each student's Educational Statement identified them as having a learning disability. Their mental health condition had been identified by the consultant psychiatrist and they attended regular appointments at his clinic. Two additional screening tools were used to examine features of the student's diagnosis and to check their level of communication. The Child and Adolescent Psychiatric Assessment Schedule (ChA-PAS) (Moss, Friedlander and Lee, 2007) is a clinical assessment of mental health problems for children and adolescents with learning disabilities. It identified that the seven students involved in the project had features of anxiety, obsessive compulsive traits and depression. Levels of communication abilities were assessed using the Children's Communication Checklist, version 2 (CCC-2; Bishop, 2003). The CCC-2 identified that all students selected for the project had a clinically significant communication problem.

Each of the seven students involved had their own individual styles of communicating. The essence of this project was about inclusion, participation and being heard, therefore interviews with the young people formed an important stage to this research. Developing an understanding of their communication patterns was essential to ensure the project meaningfully included students through tailored communication and not in a tokenistic manner merely through their presence within the project. Considering how to communicate with the participants within the chosen project of enquiry was essential to promote engagement and make the findings of the project meaningful and valid.

Tools for gathering information

Practitioners gather and act on information in their everyday roles and undoubtedly use creative approaches to find optimal methods of interacting with children who are emerging communicators or who have unique methods of communicating. These skills are invaluable in helping practitioner researchers to gather information in student projects. In Chapter 5, the practitioner researcher will have learned about designing research using qualitative and quantitative approaches, how to blend these approaches and their individual strengths and limitations. The Voice for Choice project used a mixed methods design, which combined both qualitative and quantitative approaches using observations, questionnaires and interviews.

Observations

As the Voice for Choice project aimed to develop resources to facilitate choice-making, it was important at the outset to understand the students' daily routines, establish their preferences for communicating and consider opportunities provided to them to make choices and the level of participation they had in these choices. Conducting observations early in the process of this research enabled rich, detailed information to be gathered and also prompted new ideas which were built into the research. First, it is important to establish whether or not the target information to be collected can actually be observed. For example, thoughts, feelings or attitudes cannot be observed but it is possible to observe behaviours and how people act and interact within particular situations. Another important factor at this stage is to consider the situations in which it is possible or ethical to conduct observations. Ethics and the involvement of people in research are considered in greater detail in Chapter 4 but are an essential component at every stage of the research process. In the Voice for Choice Project a consideration of ethical issues provided for obtaining informed consent from parents and, where possible, the students themselves, ensuring that students understood they had the right to withdraw from the process at any point, minimizing any disruptions and changes to established routines or indeed continuing with any newly introduced routines which were discovered to be advantageous to the student and being sensitive to any invasion of privacy during observations. Snelgrove (2005) highlights some of the ethical issues which can arise when involving individuals with learning disabilities in research, emphasizing the value of being intuitive to students' wishes and interpreting their responses ethically. Observations fall into two broad categories: laboratory and naturalistic. The term 'laboratory' is used to describe a situation where the environment is controlled, e.g. it may be possible to consider setting up a particular room to see how children respond to particular activities. In that room the practitioner can control the contents, layout, noise levels and distractions. The benefit of this is that there is more certainty about the effect that activities are having on the child's behaviour, and that these changes are less likely to be a result of other variables such as toys in the room. Pepler and Craig (1995) outline how this approach can provide good control in studies observing children; however, this may not be representative of the child's everyday interactions. While there are clear benefits of using this type of observation, it was felt that a more naturalistic approach to observing students within their own existing environment would produce better information for this project.

Naturalistic observations

Naturalistic observations literally involve the observation of individuals in their natural environments. This approach was chosen in preference to laboratory observations because the Voice for Choice project was focused on developing resources that would be used in a student's everyday education, care and therapeutic settings, therefore it was more appropriate to conduct observations in these natural environments. Despite not having full control over outside variables in the environment, as would be the case in a laboratory observation, this approach does lend itself to gathering rich, real-life information of how people behave. Observations of naturally occurring behaviour are often preferable to information gathered through interview. If asked about their behaviour, individuals may choose to answer in ways which are socially more acceptable but are not a true reflection of what actually occurs. It is also worth noting that many actions and behaviours occur subconsciously so that an individual would not necessarily report these in an interview. For example, students were observed in a classroom setting to identify the choice-making opportunities offered to them. It was noted that staff were often observed to make choices for the student without actually realizing they were doing so. An interview question about this behaviour might have elicited a different response to the observation information. As such, it was possible to build this information into the research to provide feedback and recommendations to staff in the classroom.

Naturalistic observations can be conducted in three ways:

- *Casual (unstructured, indirect) observation.* Specific situations are observed to identify what is happening, what types of behaviour are occurring and how individuals are interacting. A record of observations is made, usually from a vantage point at the rear of the classroom, but the practitioner researcher is not directly involved in the setting.
- *Systematic (structured, formal) observation.* Specific situations are observed against a pre-determined set of descriptions of behaviours, e.g. observing and taking note of choices which are offered to a particular student in a class, and how these are offered. Again, the practitioner research is not directly involved in the activities observed.
- *Participant observation (field research).* Specific situations are observed with the practitioner researcher taking an active role in sharing the experience. For example, a practitioner researcher may observe choice-making activities within their own classroom, taking an active role in the activity.

Naturally, some challenges in remaining objective will occur in situations familiar to the practitioner researcher. The mere presence of an individual in an unfamiliar setting may give rise to changes in behaviour as a result of their presence. This effect is referred to as demand characteristics (Orne, 1962). To minimize the impact of demand characteristics in the Voice for Choice project, lengthy observations were conducted with the students so that they became accustomed to the presence of the practitioner researcher. This initially involved the practitioner researcher observing from a distance to remain as unobtrusive as possible. However, as children with autism prefer their environment to be predictable and consistent, their natural curiosity prevented this from working effectively and the presence of the practitioner researcher was readily detected.

Questionnaires

The Voice for Choice project used questionnaires to gather information about the communication aids and resources used in the classrooms from members of staff working with the young people. Questionnaires are an effective way of gathering a wide range of views and information about a subject in a short period of time. This was an important consideration for the project as some of the other data collection approaches were much more time-consuming and it is important for practitioner researchers to make sure a project is viable in terms of the time needed to complete it. When designing questionnaires it is important to consider carefully the type of information needed. A questionnaire may already have been designed which has been used by others and has been established as being reliable and valid. This means that it gathers the type of information you want and can be repeated by others. However, there may be occasions where there are no standard questionnaires available and the practitioner researcher must design their own. This was the case with the Voice for Choice project which sought to gather information specific to the types of resources being designed.

In designing the questionnaire it was important to decide on the type of data to be collected. Questionnaires can be designed with the following features:

- *Open-ended questions*: these questions allow the respondent to provide their own views/answers.
- *Closed-ended questions*: these questions are followed by a fixed multiple choice or yes/no response.
- *Ranked responses*: these questions offer respondents a set of options to choose from depending on order of preference or importance.
- *Rating responses*: these questions enable respondents to choose from a set of responses about a statement and usually contain choices such as: strongly agree, agree, disagree or strongly disagree. In this case respondents circle their most appropriate choice. Sometimes the same choices are presented on a horizontal line representing a scale between two end points (e.g. agree to disagree) and respondents are asked to mark on the line their level of agreement to a particular statement.

The questionnaire designed for the Voice for Choice project sought to find out how useful traditional communication aids and resources were to practitioners working with children with learning disabilities and communication difficulties. It was decided this information would best be gathered using a combination of questions with rating responses mixed with some open-ended questions. This enabled people working with the students to give an opinion on how useful the resources were rather than merely agreeing or disagreeing with their usefulness. By including some open-ended questions at the end of the questionnaire, it was possible to gather initial impressions from staff in more detail and allow them to make recommendations about how the resources would be used.

In order to ensure a good return rate on questionnaires, research practitioners must be aware of the limitations of this method of collecting information and how to overcome them. Questionnaires designed for the Voice for Choice project tried to minimize the use of jargon terminology and presented questions in a language which was familiar to practitioners. This ensured that people were easily able to understand the questions being asked. The first few questions were designed to be engaging and non-threatening which helped to make the questionnaire more appealing to respondents In addition, to maximize the return rate, questionnaires were handed to each practitioner with an explanation given verbally of what was required. This ensured that respondents had clear instructions as to why they were completing the questionnaire and what the information will be used for. The questionnaires were also anonymous to reassure respondents that their answers would not be identifiable, thus encouraging them to be more open and honest in the opinions given.

Before the questionnaire was circulated, it was initially tested out with a group of practitioners similar to the practitioners who would be involved in the final data collection. This process helped to identify any questions which were unclear or unnecessary. This 'piloting' of questionnaires is an important step in ensuring the final questionnaire is as robust as possible. Boynton (2004) describes how trialling your questionnaire with participants who are representative of the sample in your enquiry can provide you with feedback on how people react to the questionnaire, how long it takes to complete, identify any readability issues and allow you to test out how you will administer, collect and score the questionnaire

Interviews

Interviews were used in the Voice for Choice project to develop an understanding of how the young people communicated, e.g. their choice-making opportunities and, second, to establish knowledge, facts and views about the use of resources which were developed during the research. Individual interviews were conducted with the young people and also with their education and care staff. Interviewing is a method of data collection whereby you ask a person directly for information. Barker, Pistrang and Elliott (2002) describe interviews as collecting information through 'a special type of conversation'. This method allows for the exploration of particular issues from the point of view of the person being interviewed, and gathers information about their experiences. Interviews have the advantage of being able to discuss in depth information on a topic, including facts, knowledge, opinions, values and feelings. However, the disadvantage is that they can be time-consuming to conduct as each person must be interviewed individually with their conversation being recorded to gain a true record of its meaning. Interviews then need to be typed up, verified and analysed. The information gathered may also be susceptible to practitioner bias, i.e. the tendency to influence the direction of the questions asked during the interview and how this is interpreted as a result of preference of practitioners. Johnson (1997) puts this simply as researchers 'finding what they want to find'. One way to avoid these difficulties is to ensure that particular attention is paid to the design of questions that are included in the interview schedule. These must enable the information captured to be focused and to answer the original research question.

There are two approaches to interviews:

- *structured*: an interview schedule of predetermined questions is prepared and this is rigorously adhered to;
- *unstructured*: an interview schedule of questions is prepared but these are approached flexibly enabling information generated during the interview to influence the direction of the questioning. This allows rich and valuable information to emerge during the process.

Both types of interview were used in the Voice for Choice project. Interviews with practitioners used a structured approach incorporating a checklist of questions and data was recorded by making notes on a prepared answer sheet during the interview. An unstructured approach was adopted when involving the students in interviews. These interviews were highly interactive and informal, and involved writing notes after the interview, recording the interview with a digital voice recorder or taking photographs of resources being used. These two approaches allowed the project to collect the information required but in ways which were sensitive to those involved. In designing an interview to involve the students it was important to consider individual preferences with regards to communication, and to ensure the most appropriate and reliable methods were employed. A flexible approach was used and tailored to the individual using either verbal language, signing, pictures or symbols. Lewis and Porter (2007) describe the need for practitioner researchers to be flexible and imaginative in research with children with disabilities in order to minimize difficulties which could impact on the research. Careful consideration also needed to be given with regards to how this data was recorded. Where students had verbal communication skills, a digital recording of their responses was made and subsequently typed up. Where students were emerging communicators using symbols, photos or signing, a record was made of their responses by the research practitioner and a report written immediately after the interview was concluded. Recorded responses were reported in 'verbatim' using the words and language of students to avoid misinterpretation of responses and to avoid disempowerment of an individual voice. These voices were used when the research findings were shared with others.

To help students participate fully in the interview process a range of different communication techniques were used. Where students are emerging communicators, it is very important to pay particular attention to personalized communication methods as spoken interviews are highly unlikely to provide valid information. The following types of communication were employed to interview students.

Communication systems

Augmentative and Alternative Communication

Augmentative and Alternative Communication (AAC) is a term used for communication methods which support or replace spoken language, such as gestures, sign language, pictures, symbols and computer systems with synthesized speech. The Voice for Choice project made use of symbols, Picture Exchange Communication (PECS) and Talking Mats (see below). Speech and language therapists within the organization were consulted for advice on how to use these AAC approaches effectively and the following section will outline the communication methods used by the young people within the Voice for Choice research. Before using any of these approaches it is important that a good working knowledge is obtained in order to build the techniques into any prospective research and it is recommended that advice from speech and language therapists be sought.

Symbols

Symbols can be used to replace spoken language with a visual (manual or graphic) representation of an object, word or concept. DeLoache (2004) describes how symbols can be printed words, pictures, images or objects (to name a few) which stand for something. Symbols can be used to convey single ideas or meanings, or to translate written words and symbol software packages can be purchased for this purpose. This project used the Writing with Symbols package as this was used within the host organization and by the students in their daily environment; however, it is recommended that if symbols are to be used in any research, it is important to use symbols which the students are familiar with or those which are used and familiar within the organization.

Picture Exchange Communication System

The Picture Exchange Communication System (PECS) is described as 'a unique AAC training package developed for use with young children with autism and other social-communication deficits' (Bondy and Frost, 1994) and uses a behavioural approach to initiate and support functional communication. Individuals are taught to exchange pictures for their desired item, and receiving the desired item straight away directly reinforces the exchange.

Talking Mats

Talking Mats was designed as a communication system which enables concrete responses to be given by placing symbols or picture under categories such as 'like' or 'dislike' on a mat. This method has been demonstrated as a positive means of improving attention and interaction during communications with individuals with learning disabilities (Murphy and Cameron, 2008). These authors also identify a number of factors which were taken into account while planning the Voice for Choice project, including physical factors (are there any physical or visual disabilities or impairments which may hinder the individual engaging?), distractions (the environment should be as free from distractions as possible), and motor control (does the individual have sufficient control over their motor movements and coordination to manipulate the symbols on the mat?). One issue, which could affect the validity of using Talking Mats, includes researcher bias. Practitioner researcher bias has already been discussed, however this was an important consideration in using Talking Mats to ensure that the research evidence was not biased by the researcher's own interpretations of the meaning of what was conveyed using the mats. It is useful to have someone available to conduct an objective observation of what evidence is generated by the Talking Mat process so that researcher bias does not become an issue which reduces the validity of the research. Within the Voice for Choice project, extensive liaising with speech and language therapists while using Talking Mats increased the robust nature of the data.

Puppets

One of the young people communicated verbally and engaged in much spoken conversations. However, much of his conversation was described within fantasies and stories. This created some challenges in engaging him in conversations about choice-making. When looking through his notes it was evident that previous practitioners had successfully used puppets with this young person. Using puppets to communicate with children is a technique which has been used predominantly in child therapies. Simon, Naylor, Keogh, Maloney and Downing (2008) conducted classroom-based research using puppetry as a learning tool. They concluded that using puppets in the classroom can increase engagement, motivation, listening and sharing of ideas.

The importance of good communication

Being flexible about the communication styles used in this project was essential in order to meaningfully engage with the young people and gather accurate data. When using various AACs in an enquiry project, it is important to plan ahead to anticipate all of the symbols/pictures/signs that may be required. With any new mode of communication, ethics should again be considered and the impact that these methods may have on the individuals' communication style. If a particular communication approach has been introduced or 'taught' for the purpose of research, it should not be withdrawn at the end of research as this may result in deprivation or deskilling the individual of an established method of communication. Bondy (2001) stresses this idea, stating the importance of maintaining any established method to prevent the individual losing their current skills. It is also important to consider the frequency with which participants are getting exposure to or practice of using these approaches in between research sessions. An individual's level of skill in using these techniques may affect the quality of the data collected. For example, a student who has been using Talking Mats within therapy sessions for 12 months and is familiar with this interaction style may be able to provide more detailed, and perhaps more reliable data, than someone who has been introduced to the method a few weeks prior to data collection.

Challenges to information gathering

Bias effects

Social desirability is a term used to describe how an interviewee's response may be influenced by their perception of acceptable/desirable answers as opposed to expressing their true feelings (Crowne and Marlowe, 1960). This may result in responses, which represent them in a more favourable light with the interviewer or responding in a way which they believe to be pleasing to the interviewer. Asking leading questions such as 'Did this resource help the student make a choice?' may have been more prone to bias rather than including a more neutral question such as 'Could you tell me how the student used this resource to make a choice?' Planning and preparation with regard to questions contained in interviews or a questionnaire are essential to minimize the effects of social desirability. The use of anonymous questionnaires minimizes the effects of social desirability but compromises the ability of the practitioner researcher to be able to track respondents or to identify the potential for follow-up interviews. Acquiescence bias was particularly important to consider in the Voice for Choice project. Children with disabilities and communication difficulties are particularly prone to responses that follow a pattern of answers. Respondents may answer questions in a consistently agreeable style or by consistently choosing the last option (Gilbert, 2004). This may be due to impairment affecting their understanding of the question or by aiming to please the researcher by giving a 'positive answer'. It is suggested that individuals with learning disabilities are prone to acquiesce in an effort to please the interviewer or say the 'right' or 'correct' answer; indeed, Stalker (1998) suggested this may be due to having little control over their own lives.

Researcher bias may also affect the findings of a project. This occurs when a practitioner researcher's own preferences, goals and interpretation of information/situations has an effect on the way data is collected. For example, the Voice for Choice project used a variety of data collection approaches. Had the project relied solely on unstructured interviews, the practitioner researcher might have unintentionally influenced the questioning to gather information on the positive aspects of resources, which had been designed, rather than allowing for consideration of areas of difficulty. This might have led to inaccurate results.

Trusting the information gathered

When any information is gathered and reported, readers must be confident that the results are reliable and, where possible, they can use the information to inform their own practice. Information gathered must be reliable and valid. Reliability and validity are terms used extensively in collecting information. Reliability refers to the ability to collect information, which can be repeated to give the same result (Dyer, 2007). The term validity refers to whether research is measuring what it is intended to and is important to assess the extent that findings and conclusions from research are justified (Dyer, 2007). A key approach to mitigate against bias and strengthen reliability and validity of information gathered is the use of triangulation.

Triangulation

Triangulation is defined by Denzin (1978, p. 602) as 'the combination methodologies in the study of the same phenomenon'. It is a method to ensure your inquiry has higher levels of reliability and validity. The Voice for Choice project used different approaches to collect information through observations, questionnaires and interviews. This information then provided evidence from different perspectives on the same issue. For example, during the Voice for Choice project, one of the resources designed and trialled was a communication card. The communication card contains brief, key information on how an individual chooses to communicate, with phrases to encourage the health professional to engage with them (e.g. 'Please remember I am listening' or 'Please involve me'). The purpose of this card was to increase dialogue and positive interaction in health consultations, directly between the individual and the health professional. Extensive trialling of this resource was not possible during the timescale of the project, as there were only limited opportunities to observe health appointments. However, to gather robust evidence on the ways in which this resource benefitted the young person, a variety of methods were used to collect evidence from multiple perspectives. The views of the young person were gathered through interviews (verbally, supported with Talking Mats); views of members of staff working with him were gathered through questionnaires; and also any changes in behaviour before, during and after health appointments were observed and noted. These three sets of evidence were then analysed, looking for similar patterns and also inconsistencies in this instance. Triangulation of this information provided consistent conclusions about the benefits of the communication card. This approach avoids basing findings on just one perspective and can also help by highlighting any sets of data which may have been biased by particular factors and may need further investigation.

Conclusion

A number of data collection methods have been presented in this chapter, including a discussion of strengths, limitations and benefits of using mixed methods designs. It is important to consider these strengths and limitations when planning an inquiry project keeping in mind how suitable these methods may be for engaging and meaningfully including young people. Thorough planning and pilot studies will help to identify potential sources of error and biases, allowing practitioner researchers to adjust and improve their investigation. Choosing the most appropriate methodology will offer opportunities to gather information, which is more accurate, enabling more reliable conclusions to be drawn which can be shared confidently with others.

Using a mixed methods design has the advantage of including all the strengths of each of these methods in your investigation. The Voice for Choice project included the rich in-depth information from interviews, with a large quantity of information from questionnaires and also situational, real-life information from observations. In addition to these advantages, using mixed methods and triangulating the information allowed the practitioner researcher to compare themes from the evidence to support robust valid and reliable findings.

Offering information, choice and involving individuals who have learning and communicative difficulties can be challenging. By creating the appropriate environment and using meaningful approaches, individuals with varying communication problems can be included in a project and research practitioners can provide valid support for innovative ways of working to promote positive outcomes for all students.

Note

1   Physical interventions are defined as 'A method of responding to the challenging behaviour of people with learning disability and/or autism which involves some degree of direct physical force which limits or restricts the movement or mobility of the person concerned' (British Institute of Learning Difficulties, 2010).

References

Barker, C., Pistrang, N. and Elliott, R. (2002) *Research Methods in Clinical Psychology*, 2nd edn. Chichester: John Wiley & Sons, Ltd.

Bishop, D.V.M. (2003) *The Children's Communication Checklist, version 2 (CCC-2)*. London: Pearson Assessment.

Bondy, A. (2001) PECS: potential benefits and risks. *The Behaviour Analyst Today* 2(2), 127–132.

Bondy, A. and Frost, L. (1994) The picture exchange communication system. *Focus on Autistic Behaviour*, 11, 1–19.

Boynton, P. (2004) Administering, analysing, and reporting your questionnaire. *British Medical Journal*, 329(7461), 1372–1375.

British Institute of Learning Difficulties (2010) *Code of Practice for the Use and Reduction of Restrictive Physical Interventions.* Kidderminster: BILD Publications.

Clark, E., Olympia, D., Jensen, J., Heathfield, L. and Jenson, W. (2003) Striving for autonomy in a contingency-governed world: another challenge for individuals with developmental disabilities. *Psychology in the Schools*, 41(1), 143–153.

Crowne, D.P. and Marlowe, D. (1960) A new scale of social desirability independent of psychopathology. *Journal of Consulting Psychology*, 24(4) 349–354.

DeLoache, J.S. (2004) Becoming symbol minded. *Trends in Cognitive Sciences*, 8(2), 66–70.

Denzin, N.K (1978) *The Research Act*, 2nd edition. New York: McGraw-Hill. Cited in Jick, T.D. (1978) Mixing qualitative and quantitative methods: triangulation in action. *Administrative Science Quarterly*, 24(4), 602–611.

Dyer, C. (2007) *Research in Psychology: A Practical Guide to Methods and Statistics.* Oxford: Blackwell Publishing.

Foundation for People with Learning Disabilities (2001) *Count Us In: The Report of the Committee of Inquiry into Meeting the Mental Health Needs of Young People with Learning Disabilities.* London: Mental Health Foundation.

Gilbert, T. (2004) Involving people with learning disabilities in research: issues and possibilities. *Health and Social Care in the Community*, 12(4), 298–308.

Johnson, R.B. (1997) Examining the validity structure of qualitative research. *Education*, 118(2), 282–292.

Lewis, A. and Porter, J. (2007) Research and pupil voice. In L. Florian (ed.) *Handbook of Special Education.* London: Sage.

Moss, S., Friedlander, R. and Lee, P. (2007) *The Cha-PAS Interview for the Assessment of Mental Health in Children and Adolescents.* Brighton: Pavilion Publishing.

Murphy, J. and Cameron, L. (2008) The effectiveness of Talking Mats® with people with intellectual disability. *British Journal of Learning Disabilities*, 36(4), 232–241.

Orne, M.T. (1962) On the social psychology of the psychological experiment: with particular reference to demand characteristics and their implications. *American Psychologist*, 17(11), 776–783.

Pepler, D.J. and Craig, W.M. (1995) A peek behind the fence: naturalistic observations of aggressive children with remote audiovisual recording. *Developmental Psychology*, 13(4), 548–553.

Porter, J. (2003) Interviewing children and young people with learning disabilities. *The SLD Experience*, 36, 14–17.

Simon, S., Naylor, S., Keogh, B., Maloney, J. and Downing, B. (2008) Puppets promoting engagement and talk in science. *International Journal of Science Education*, 30(9), 1229–1248.

Snelgrove, S. (2005) Bad, mad and sad: Developing a methodology of inclusion and a pedagogy for researching students with intellectual disabilities. *International Journal of Inclusive Education*, 9(3), 313–329.

Stalker, K. (1998) Some ethical and methodological issues in research with people with learning difficulties. *Disability and Society*, 13(1), 5–19.

Chapter 7

Making sense of data

An analysis of alternate assessment

Katherine Hawley

Introduction

Melissa is a middle school teacher within a self-contained classroom for students with intellectual disabilities in a large school district in Southwest Florida. She is carrying out a project on teachers' perceptions of a newly implemented state alternate assessment for students who have severe intellectual disabilities. She has developed her inquiry questions based on what she wants to know, read what others have written about alternate assessment, explored some of the possible approaches to carry out her project, received informed consent, and has collected teacher data through surveys. Now, she is overwhelmed with the amount of information she has generated. There are piles of completed surveys strewn around her dining room floor. She is wondering how she is going to make sense of it all!

There are many ways in which practitioners can organize the data they have collected through an inquiry project. This chapter will provide an overview of different ways to do this in the context of school-based inquiry, and will then focus on the strategies that Melissa, a teacher used to investigate teachers' perceptions of the newly implemented state alternate assessment process (the "Alternate Assessment Project"), used. The chapter will share how Melissa accomplished this in a way that connected back to key questions that framed the inquiry and the reading of what others had written about alternate assessment. The chapter also discusses the associated challenges that a practitioner may face in analysing data together with potential strategies that can be employed to overcome such challenges.

At the end of this chapter, practitioners will have a stronger understanding of how to manage and make sense of collected data, and be aware of specific strategies that can assist with interpretation. This stage of the ARC cycle focuses on how a practitioner makes sense of gathered data. It is concerned with how to manage and interpret data. The intention of this stage of the ARC is to analyze data in a meaningful way, whilst paying attention to how the process of interpretation truly represents the teachers' perspectives (validity) and to a lesser extent, how other practitioner/researchers can use the same process of analysis and reach similar interpretations (reliability). Data analysis can be one of the most over-whelming components of the ARC.

It is important to have a structured action plan relating to how emerging data will be managed and interpreted. It needs to be set at the beginning of the ARC. If the practitioner waits until all the data is collected, then sets out to create an action plan on data analysis, the practitioner may come upon unforeseen consequences, including gaps in the data or the wrong data were collected.

Before a practitioner can begin to analyze the data, they must have a set plan on how to organize the data. To begin, the practitioner must first convert the raw data into a useful form. For qualitative data, a practitioner needs to use the following continuum techniques: coding data by assigning numeric values into a codebook, cleaning the database for errors, recoding or computing new variables for computer analysis (Creswell & Clark, 2007). New variables would need to be identified and introduced as part of the ongoing process, and then the coding would need to be rechecked. SPSS and SAS are two statistical computer pro-grams that can be used for recoding and statistical computing purposes. However, practitioners can carry out the same procedures that computer programs can produce by either hand coding the data set or by using a simple spreadsheet computer application.

For qualitative data, a practitioner can use these techniques: organizing docu-ments and visual data, transcribing interview data into a word document, and then transferring it into a "qualitative data analysis software program, such as MAXqda, Atlas.ti., NVivo, or HyperRESEARCH" (Creswell & Clark, 2007, p. 130). Practitioners also have the option of bypassing computer programs and choosing to complete the process by hand. Choosing which type of method to organize data depends on what type of data was collected during a study (Creswell & Clark, 2007). For the purposes of this study, the practitioner could have used colored coded highlighting based on themes or a qualitative data analysis software program, but chose to transcribe the qualitative responses onto individual index cards.

The Alternate Assessment Project

The Alternate Assessment Project grew from the implementation of a new state-level alternate assessment tool for students with severe disabilities. Federal man-dates, specifically The No Child Left Behind Act (2002), require that all students demonstrate adequate yearly progress and must be assessed in reading, math, and science. This is referred to as statewide accountability. However, students who have the grade-level content standards modified through their Individual Education Plan (IEP) are eligible to be assessed with an alternate assessment based on modified academic achievement standards under Federal regulation 34 C.F.R. Part 200. The Federal government does not endorse or specify a single alternate assessment tool; therefore, each state is free to develop their own alter-nate assessments (Byrnes, 2004).

Alternate assessments are a relatively new educational initiative, with a growing evidence base. The majority of the emerging research on teachers' perceptions is based upon one state's alternate assessment approach (Kentucky Alternate Portfolio), which is considered one of the most established alternate assessment approaches in the US (Roach, Elliott, & Berndt, 2007). Research indicates a general theme that teachers perceive a range of benefits when including students with the most significant cognitive disabilities in statewide accountability systems (Flowers, Ahlgrim-Delzell, Browder, & Spooner, 2005; Kampfer, Horvath, Kleinert, & Kearns, 2001; Kleinert, Kennedy, & Farmer Kearns, 1999). However, teachers have also expressed concerns with the amount of time required to complete alternate assessments (Flowers et al., 2005; Roach, Elliott, & Berndt, 2007). Flowers, Browder, Wakeman, and Karvonen (2006) suggest that most teachers believe this population of students should be included in school and district accountability systems. Towles-Reeves, Kleinert, and Muhomba (2009) state that there is limited research on the implications of how alternate assessments alter classroom and school-level practices. As a result, Melissa was interested in exploring teachers' perceptions of a newly adopted alternate assessment in her state and the perceived impact upon actual classroom practices.

The newly implemented alternate assessment (FAA) is a performance-based instrument based on modified general education standards. The Teacher Perception Project examined the perceptions of special education teachers, specifically related to the effectiveness of the instrument, the impact on instructional practices, any policy implications and emerging professional development issues. In the spirit of practitioner research, one of the goals of this project was to increase Melissa's understanding and skills in classroom practice (Gall, Gall, & Borg, 2007).

According to Creswell and Clark (2007), "rigorous research designs are important because they guide the methods decisions that researchers must make during their studies and set the logic by which they make interpretations at the end of studies" (p. 58). Melissa decided upon a mixed methods triangulation design that consisted of an embedded approach (Creswell & Clark, 2007). Melissa was interested in finding out about statistical patterns as well as hearing teachers' stories of their experiences of the new alternate assessment. She designed a closed and open-ended question for a survey that had four sections: demographics; strengths and weaknesses of the alternate assessment; effective measure of student progress; and policy and instructional implications, with a total of 36 questions. She designed the survey to be completed online. Of the 36 questions, 25 of the questions were Likert scale-style questions with a rating scale of strongly agree, agree, undecided, disagree, and strongly disagree. The Likert scale questions also included space for teachers to provide qualitative information in the form of how and why questions. In her design, Melissa utilized a concurrent timing approach where the quantitative and qualitative data were collected simultaneously. Tashkkori and Teddlie (2003) support her research design by affirming that the collection and analysis of qualitative and quantitative data provide an in-depth picture of teachers' perspectives while also demonstrating statistical patterns in the data.

The Alternate Assessment Project involved teachers of students with severe disabilities from five different counties in the state of Florida in the USA. Teachers were contacted through the state website. One hundred and sixteen teachers, out of a possible 180 who were contacted, completed the online survey from this convenience sample. Each participant was given an identification number that would assist in the data analysis and help ensure participant anonymity.

How to make sense of the information gathered?

One hundred and sixteen teachers completed the surveys, creating a vast amount of data. It is vital to have a clear plan relating to how to organize the data and process the information, while ensuring the highest levels of validity and reliability. It is helpful to set this plan before any data is collected. Validity refers to "the degree to which a thing measures what it reports to measure" (Johnson, 2005, p. 82). The Alternate Assessment Project needed to make sure that the measurement instrument yielded data that actually measured what it said it was going to measure. Furthermore, attention needed to be paid to creating greater levels of reliability, or "the degree to which a study or experiment can be repeated with similar results" (Johnson, 2005, p. 83). Would the Alternate Assessment Project receive the same results if repeated in another state or country? To assist with the management of the data, a four-step process for data management was adopted:

Stage 1: Likert scale questions were quantitatively analyzed to find means and standard deviations.

Stage 2: Qualitative responses were initially coded for major themes by the teacher, and then the process was repeated by a colleague.

Stage 3: Major themes were analyzed for a second time by both teachers, subthemes were developed and raw data attributed to each subtheme.

Stage 4: A "Grounded Methods" approach was utilized to connect the emerging themes with literature in the field (Gall, Gall, & Borg, 2007).

At each stage, seven questions were posed:

1   How can the data be interpreted?
2   How can greater levels of validity be achieved?
3   How can greater levels of reliability be achieved?
4   How can results be presented in a simple way that supports clear appreciation of the data and subsequent analysis?
5   How can data be presented in a way that shows meaning making?

6   Where are the links back to the literature and is there a need to carry out a further literature search?

7   How can data analysis be presented in a way that relates the current findings and insights to initial research questions and also highlight the links back to the literature base?

How can the data be interpreted?

In the Alternate Assessment Project it was important to find "the story" that the teachers' responses were telling. Initially, the analysis of individual question responses became subordinate to the overall "story" of all the responses. A mixed methods triangulation analysis was applied where the qualitative and quantitative data was analyzed concurrently.

First, quantitative analysis of the Likert scale questions occurred by calculating the means and standard deviations for each question. The focus was upon any emerging patterns from the quantitative data. Next, the qualitative data was analyzed. The first step in analyzing qualitative data is to code the data, or divide the responses into small units, such as phrases, sentences, or paragraphs (Creswell & Clark, 2007). In the Alternate Assessment Project it was decided to take a hands-on approach. Each qualitative response (exact words from the data were used) was placed on an index card, including the participant ID number. The response index cards were then grouped into initial major themes on large sheets of paper.

How can greater levels of validity be achieved?

Validity refers "to the extent to which the instruments are measuring what they are supposed to be measuring" (Orcher, 2005, p. 53). Several methods could be used to increase the validity of a project: member checking, triangulation, reporting disconfirming evidence, and internal validation (Cresswell & Clark, 2007). Member checking consists of bringing the interpretations of the results back to a sample of the participants to see if they believe the interpretations are a true meaning of the study's intention (Orcher, 2005). Researchers can also use triangulation of data sources to ensure greater levels of validity. This consists of the researcher using more than one type of source for data (Orcher, 2005). "Disconfirming evidence is information that presents a perspective that is contrary to the one indicated by the established evidence" (Cresswell & Clark, 2007, p. 135). For the Alternate Assessment Project, an internal validation process by a second researcher was adopted. This process entails a second researcher, who is familiar with qualitative research as well as the content area of the research project, reviewing the data and analysis. The second researcher in the project was experienced in the field of special education, specifically inclusionary practices and assessment for students with significant cognitive disabilities. During this process, patterns of shared interpretation of data emerge and opportunities to discuss different interpretations occur. Cresswell and Clark (2007) call this procedure inter-coder agreement. It is through this discussion that a stronger level of internal validity can be achieved.

How can greater levels of reliability be achieved?

Reliability deals with "the extent to which results are consistent" (Orcher, 2005, p. 54) and "to the degree to which a measurement can be replicated" (Hunter & Brewer, 2003, p. 581). Reliability refers to the "extent to which other researchers could arrive at similar results if they studied the same case using exactly the same procedures as the first researcher" (Gall, Gall, & Borg, 2007, p. 651). In the Alternate Assessment Project, increased levels of reliability come from clarity and transparency of the collection and analysis of the data. Inter-coder agreement also increased levels of reliability in the analysis of data.

How can results be presented in a simple way that supports clear appreciation of the data and subsequent analysis?

In the Alternate Assessment Project, when all of the qualitative data and quantitative data were grouped into major themes and measures to improve levels of validity were implemented, it was time to consider ways to present the results in a simple way. Twenty-one themes were generated in the data analysis and it became increasingly apparent that these were too many to make sense to someone outside of the project. The amount of themes impacted the ability to extract the teachers' stories. Therefore, both researchers returned to the data analysis, and developed global themes by collapsing together the already established 21 themes. From this process eight global themes emerged that represented the 21 subthemes. Figure 7.1 demonstrates how these eight global themes were graphically organized

How can data be presented in a way that shows meaning making?

Once the data was analyzed into the eight major themes, the "story" of the teachers' perceptions in relation to the theme was further analyzed. In other words, how do the qualitative responses support, affirm, or challenge the quantitative interpretations?

Tables for each theme were created that presented information about the number of teachers who made comments related to that theme, the total number of comments that were made related to the theme, and specific quotes from the data that supported the theme. Table 7.1 demonstrates one of the global themes that was extracted from the analysis.

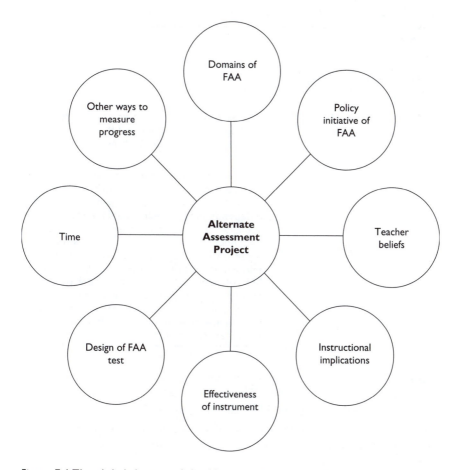

Figure 7.1 The global themes of the Alternate Assessment Project

Once this was completed for each theme, a process was needed to represent how the qualitative responses support, affirm, or challenge the quantitative responses. It was decided to create a table that presents the emerging stories from the quantitative data. Table 7.2 demonstrates emerging stories from the teachers' responses of the Likert scale questions.

Most teachers conducting research through the ARC process will not have access to the amount of respondents that the Alternate Assessment Project was able to include. When this is the case, it is important to know that practitioners do not need to use percentages when displaying results. With smaller sample sizes comes more non-generalizability of the data collected. However, the themes yielded from such data can be of interest to other populations that share similar characteristics.

Table 7.1 Global theme 1: domains of FAA

Number of respondents commented in relation to theme (n = 116)	Number of total comments (n = 761)	Examples
48 (41%)	128 (17%)	It does NOT measure anything outside of reading, math, and science. Life for our students is about SO much more than that. (54)
		The test is only measuring academic components while working with students in a center; there is so much we work on, i.e. independent functioning, communication, and social skills. For our children that will be dependent most of their lives and will be living with a caregiver. I believe it is very important that they learn life skills to the best of their ability. Being able to grow academically is great but it is much more important that they learn not to hurt others, participate in leisure activity, communicate their needs, etc. (110)

Table 7.2 Emergent stories from Likert scale questions

The measurement of progress for this group of students:

82% of teachers reported there are other ways to measure progress.

55% of teachers reported the FAA (pilot) is not an effective way to measure progress.

63% of teachers reported the FAA (pilot) not a reliable measure of progress.

64% of teachers reported the FAA does not present an accurate picture of student achievement.

Where are the links back to the literature and is there a need to carry out a further literature search?

The next step in analysis of data is to connect the findings to the literature base. A grounded theory approach links the literature to the study findings. According to Glaser and Strauss (1967), grounded theory is "the discovery of theory from data" and "provides us with relevant predictions, explanations, interpretations, and applications" (p. 1). Gall, Gall, and Borg (2007) define grounded theory as "an approach to theory development that involves deriving constructs and laws directly from the immediate data that the researcher has collected rather than drawing on an existing data" (p. 641). This provides a comprehensive way to connect the emerging themes with literature. The Alternate Assessment Project was able to link three major interpretations from the study with alternate assessment research literature: tension between individual needs of students and items on FAA, issue of time, and evidence that some teachers have altered their instructional practices due to the implementation of the FAA. The first link with the literature relates to the tension between perceived individual needs of students with severe disabilities and items of the alternate assessment. The Alternate Assessment Project highlighted the apparent disconnect with items on the alternate assessment and classroom instruction. This was also evident in Kleinert, Kennedy, and Farmer Kearns' study (1999). The second link was the issue of time. Teachers reported time as an issue in their experience of administering the FAA that was as additionally reported by Flowers, Ahlgrim-Delzell, Browder, and Spooner (2005), and Roach, Elliott, and Berndt (2007). The third link back to the literature base consists of evidence that some teachers have altered their instructional practices due to the implementation of Alternate Assessment. The Alternate Assessment Project found evidence that some teachers have incorporated elements of the alternate assessment into daily instruction as suggested as well by Towles-Reeves and Kleinert (2006). In the Alternate Assessment Project there were clear links for three global themes. However, this left five themes that required further exploration. This subsequent literature exploration can be directed by the actual themes themselves.

How can data analysis be presented in a way that relates the current findings and insights to research questions and also highlight the links to the literature base?

The data analysis now needs to be presented in order to connect findings to the initial research questions and also link back to what others have said. In order to accomplish this step, in the Alternate Assessment Project, all the tables of data from the eight major qualitative themes, and the tables from the analysis of the quantitative responses were collated and mapped to research questions and what others have said.

Challenges in the analysis of the data

During the planning and implementation stages of the Alternate Assessment Project, there were several challenges encountered with the data analysis process. The first was how to deal with the overwhelming sheer amount of data generated from the completed surveys. There were a successfully large number of teachers who completed the survey, hence a lot of data to handle and manage. The project used an online survey program to assist with data organization. The online program allowed the electronic sorting of data, for example the qualitative responses were collated separately from the quantitative responses. This helped with data management and increased the efficiency and effectiveness of the preliminary analysis.

Another challenge with the data was related to the issue of how to present the data in a meaningful way that related to the initial questions. The piles of the unorganized, raw data were initially so overwhelming that it impacted attempts to begin making meaning of all the data. What helped tremendously was a clear and organized plan to sort through the data in a systematic way. For the Alternate Assessment Project this was done visually and supported the detection of emerging global themes. Graphic charts and tables assisted with matching data to each theme. This visual display strategy allowed the data to be managed and analyzed in a more attainable way.

Conclusion

The Alternate Assessment Project enabled insight into teachers' responses to the state initiative in standardized assessment for students with low incidence disabilities. Teachers such as Melissa need the confidence and tools to explore an issue in depth that specifically relates to their practice. This chapter has highlighted the "analysis" stage of the ARC process and has shown that although data analysis can be initially perceived as overwhelming, a systematic approach to handling managing and analyzing data is extremely beneficial. At the conclusion of the Alternate Assessment Project, which followed the stages of the ARC, the following was found:

- There was an increased understanding by teachers themselves about the role of Alternate Assessment in the schooling of students with low incidence disabilities.
- There are many benefits to hearing from other teachers who are engaged in a new initiative.
- There are many benefits to the Alternate Assessment Process.
- There were opportunities to reflect on current instructional practices and improve upon these, following the ideas given by other teachers in the state.
- There are some shared concerns that need to be fed back to district and state leaders in alternate assessment.

The project highlighted that a clear plan on how data will be organized and analyzed is the key to this stage of the ARC process. Without a clear plan, practitioners can be overwhelmed with the amount of raw data and errors of coding can occur. This can lead to a lack of validity and reliability, which is essential to the credibility of the project. Finally Melissa, who was directly involved in the new state-wide alternate assessment initiative, recognized the need to engage in inquiry that gathered the perceptions of other teachers. Through this she realized that she shared some of the same stories that emerged in the data around alternate assessments. This became particularly apparent after the visual displaying of the findings with tables and charts.

As a result of the Alternate Assessment Project, Melissa gained an appreciation of how beneficial the ARC cycle is by allowing practitioners to become researchers of their own practice. Not only did she find that the ARC cycle was accessible, but that this inquiry approach was rigorous and meaningful.

References

Byrnes, M. (2004). Alternate Assessment FAQs (and answers). *Teaching Exceptional Children*, 36(6), 58–63.

Creswell, J.W., & Clark, V.L. (2007). *Designing and conducting mixed methods research.* Thousand Oaks, CA: Sage.

Flowers, C., Ahlgrim-Delzell, L., Browder, D., & Spooner, F. (2005). Teachers' perceptions of alternate assessments. *Research & Practice for Persons with Severe Disabilities*, 30(2), 81–92.

Flowers, C., Browder, D.M., Wakeman, S., & Karvonen, M. (2006). *Alternate Assessment Alignment study: Report to State B Department of Education.* Charlotte, NC: University of North Carolina at Charlotte, National Alternate Assessment Center.

Gall, M.D., Gall, J.P., & Borg, W.R. (2007). *Educational research: An introduction*, 8th edn. Boston, MA: Pearson.

Glaser, B., & Strauss, A. (1967). *The discovery of grounded theory: Strategies for qualitative research.* Chicago: Aldine.

Hunter, A., & Brewer, J. (2003). Multimethod research in sociology. In A. Tashkkori & C. Teddlie (eds.) *Handbook of mixed methods in social and behavioral research.* Thousand Oaks, CA: Sage.

Johnson, A.P. (2005). *A short guide to action research.* Boston, MA: Pearson.

Kampfer, S., Horvath, L., Kleinert, H., & Kearns, J. (2001). Teachers' perceptions of one state's alternate assessment portfolio program: Implications for practice and preparation. *Exceptional Children*, 67, 361–374.

Kleinert, H.L., Kennedy, S., & Farmer Kearns, J. (1999). The impact of alternate assessments: A statewide teacher survey. *Journal of Special Education*, 33(2), 93–102.

Orcher, L.T. (2005). *Conducting research: Social and behavioral science methods.* Glendale, CA: Pyrczak Publishing.

Roach, A.T., Elliott, S.N., & Berndt, S. (2007). Teachers' perceptions and the consequential validity of an alternate assessment for students with significant cognitive disabilities. *Journal of Disability Policy Studies*, 18(3), 168–175.

Tashkkori, A. & Teddlie, C. (2003). *Handbook of mixed methods in social and behavioral research.* Thousand Oaks, CA: Sage.

Towles-Reeves, E., & Kleinert, H. (2006). The impact of one state's alternate assessment upon instruction and IEP development. *Rural Special Education Quarterly*, 25(3), 31–39.

Towles-Reeves, E., Kleinert, H., & Muhomba, M. (2009). Alternate assessment: Have we learned anything new? *Exceptional Children*, 75(2), 233–252.

Legislation

No Child Left Behind Act of 2002, Pub. L. No. 107–110, 115 Stat. 1425 (2002).

Chapter 8

Sharing discoveries about students' experiences of inclusive practice

Christine Klopfer

Introduction to dissemination

Dissemination means to scatter in all directions, like the blowing seeds of a dandelion catching winds aloft to share new blossoms in distant lawns. The sharing of information resulting from an inquiry is critical to the end product. Why investigate something if not to share with others, when new discoveries can be utilized or improved upon for the benefit of the students and families whom professionals serve? If a practitioner-researcher has found a strategy or method that "works," do they not have a *responsibility* to inform others? Their insights could lead to important improvements in education for students with disability labels, an historically underserved population. Practitioner-researchers who enthusiastically share their findings with others can make effective practice bloom in other contexts and classrooms. Near the end of the Accessible Research Cycle practitioner-researchers are at the stage to consider how best to share their results and insights with families and other professionals, with an eye toward further development of their research and potential publication.

Education researchers typically share information about their work through journal articles, meetings with colleagues, university courses, and conference presentations. The tedious publication process requires a great deal of time for submissions to be reviewed, changes to be made, acceptance granted, and work to be published for the findings to finally trickle down to others. The end product is typically intended for other scholars in the field, and may not be accessible in a timely, convenient, or interesting manner to teachers who may lack resources like time and money to attend conferences, purchase costly journals, or take courses.

Smith, Richards-Tutor, and Cook (2010) describe teachers as an audience disconnected from research, who may be impatient with the jargon and statistics that scholarly research reports utilize. They may feel that the researchers do not understand the classroom dynamics, so how could the findings apply? One teacher summed it up when she said, "Research is not real life" (Nelson, Leffler, & Hansen, 2009, cited in Smith, Richards-Tutor, & Cook, 2010, p. 68). So the important question becomes, how do educators receive information about new and exciting practices in a way that makes them want to put it into practice right away? Teachers at all experience levels exchange information with one another to improve their practice and develop their professional skills. This professional knowledge sharing provides a ready format for disseminating concepts to foster growth and sustainability (Mawhinney, 2009).

Shermer (2007, cited in Smith, Richards-Tutor, & Cook, 2010) describes humans as storytellers; people have to be good storytellers to share theories and information effectively. People have engaged listeners with stories throughout time, long before the written word became the standard for sharing information. Storytellers have a connection with their audience, and are known for utilizing a variety of strategies to gain and keep attention, resulting in the story being passed on to others. For effective dissemination, practitioner-researchers need to develop a collaborative relationship with their audience to create a paradigm shift in research reporting (Friese & Bogenschneider, 2009). This chapter describes how one teacher told her story of research through video vignettes and shared this story with her school community and other professionals through state conference presentations. By the end of this chapter, the reader will have discovered a variety of ways to share findings from teacher research, to understand the necessary details and implications of sharing the information, and be aware of potential problems.

A story to share

Shawna gasped as she withdrew from the wide grin and raucous greeting thrust inches from her nose. "He's saying hello, don't worry," soothes Ms. Mills. "He's very excited to see you. Brandon, did you see Shawna's face? I think she was a little nervous at the way you said hello. Let's try again in a quieter way so she understands better, like this." Ms. Mills models personal space and a softer greeting for the children and encourages Shawna to initiate a greeting to Brandon, providing a peer model that he may relate to more readily than her teacher model. The teacher fades back to observe, smiling discreet satisfaction as she reflects on the positive changes in Brandon since the beginning of the school year two months ago.

Brandon is a 7-year-old boy, one of six male students in Ms. Mills' self-contained Intermediate class for students with labels of autism. He has dual labels of autism and language impairment and a Behavior Improvement Plan designed to improve some of his less desirable behaviors, such as hitting others, spitting, and running about the classroom shouting gleefully during instructional periods. During teacher pre-service the week before school began, Ms. Mills had been cautioned about how "difficult" Brandon was to have in the classroom. In fact, he had such a litany of documentation he had been deemed unmanageable in his current placement, and was destined for the county's school of last resort for students with more significant disabilities. In this school all the students have a disability label and are grouped accordingly, so Brandon would have no opportunity to learn from students his age without disabilities. The paper trail to the placement change was nearly complete. Ms. Mills, a newly qualified teacher, knew from her recent university coursework that time with similar aged peers could provide benefits to her students that she could not directly teach (Bellini, 2006). She was determined to try some of the tools in her teacher toolbox to see if they would have a positive effect on him.

First-year teachers in her district are assigned a school-based mentor to ease the transition from university to full-time teacher. Mentors are usually veteran teachers who know the school system very well and help new teachers with everything from classroom arrangement to paperwork. Ms. Mills hadn't yet built any collaborative relationships with other teachers on campus, so she asked her mentor to help her connect with general education teachers who might be open to working together in some capacity to provide her students access to general education peers and curriculum. Mrs. Harding, a second-grade teacher with nearly 30 years' experience, eagerly stepped forward to invite Ms. Mills' class to participate with hers, and was open to how that might play out. This was where the project was born. With little time to plan, students carried messages between the teachers to share ideas and invitations to special events. Most of the interactions occurred in the larger space of Mrs. Harding's room, but the students also spent time together in Ms. Mills' class, Specialized Physical Education classes where the coach taught group games, and on the playground. Activities include shared reading, puppet theatre, games, interactive lessons, singing and movement in whole group and small group settings.

Initially, Ms. Mills considered only the benefits for her students. Eight-year-old Derek progressed from watching activities from outside the classroom door to active participation within two weeks. Peter, continually distracted by books to the point of not noticing others, became the book selector and page turner for the teacher, and could sometimes be coaxed to read aloud to the group. Brandon watched the postures and motions of his new friends carefully and soon curtailed his physical disruptions and learned to sit in a circle on the floor. Brandon was able to generalize this to sitting appropriately in his classroom and in the cafeteria, and this along with other improvements led to him staying in her class rather than moving to a more restrictive school. Other practitioners began to remark on her students' progress as they generalized school-expected behaviors throughout the day. After a fire drill one afternoon, the school principal momentarily thought she had a new student, not recognizing Brandon's calm and listening demeanor.

As they spent more time together, there seemed to be a natural progression of increased engagement between the students, the teachers, and the materials and activities. Through a camera lens, Ms. Mills narrowed her focus to the personal exchanges between the students, and noticed communication and relationships building as the students got to know one another, and learned ways to share information and help each other. Both teachers knew exciting and amazing things were happening for each and every student. Ms. Mills loved to tell the stories of

Brandon's successes, Derek and Peter's improved involvement, and the ways that Mrs. Harding's students naturally adapted their communication and interactions to scaffold for the students who did these things differently than they were used to. She soon began to feel that the developments were too important not to share with a larger audience. The question for her became how to go about helping others understand the exciting impact of her inclusion project in a way that would be accurate, accessible, and engaging enough to encourage other teachers to develop similar collaborative projects.

Dissemination methods: telling the story

Ms. Mills told anyone who would stop and listen to her enthusiastic stories of the inclusion project, but she knew that word of mouth was limiting. She wanted to find a way to share with a much wider audience and also to include the personal stories the students had to tell. She had many photographs, but decided that video vignettes would have a greater impact as well as being a more accurate reporting format. She used a small, hand-held video recorder to document interactions across the various settings, and interviewed the students as a group, being careful to put them at ease to capture their most genuine reactions. She put together an 8-minute video of a mix of activities that the students shared, with the interviews voiced over the images. As she was a novice with the movie editing program, the final product was rough, but she felt good about the messages that it carried about the activities the children had participated in, and how it showed the positive benefits of inclusion for them. Embedded in the messages were increased awareness and acceptance of ability differences and how the students learned new ways of communicating and interacting.

After explaining the purpose of the video to the children, she sent a letter home to families to describe their child's role, and methodically collected informed consent from each participant to ensure she had permission to use their voices and images. She began sharing the video, first with her teaching team, then with the teaching staff at her school. Viewers seemed captivated by the innovation and maturity displayed by the students, and remarked on their own previous perceptions of people with autism as being positively affected by watching how they participated and communicated with their peers. At the county's year-end Trans-disciplinary meeting, Ms. Mills shared the story and the video with staff from three schools and county ESE professionals. Parents viewed the video at an annual autism family breakfast, and one father commented that he saw his son in a new light, as he never considered that he could have friendships with peers without disabilities. He saw him as "just one of the guys" in the group. Every person who watched the video seemed to gain an awareness and appreciation of diversity and acceptance, and also began to see an opening for increased collaboration and inclusion efforts in their educational sphere.

The Partnership for Effective Programs for Students with Autism (PEPSA) enhances all aspects of educational programming through partnership with teachers that include mentorship, project design, implementation, and reporting, grants, and potential conference presentation. This is a state-funded program implemented through the Center for Autism and Related Disabilities (CARD). Ms. Mills had been accepted as a PEPSA Partner for that school year. She submitted the video and a paper on the collaborative inclusion project as part of the PEPSA Partner requirements, and was pleased to be chosen to present her project at CARD's next state conference in Orlando, FL. Attendees at this conference include Exceptional Student Education and general education teachers, occupational therapists, speech and language pathologists, families, students, county ESE staff, university professionals and students, and support agency staff, amongt others. The potential audience was large and varied, as this conference drew people from all over Florida. National keynote speakers and workshop presenters broadened the scope of the conference.

The presentation was well attended and received positive feedback from families, educators, and county support staff. An inclusion support specialist from another county requested more information and permission to share the video with families. For those who were at co-occurring presentations, a project board in the conference facility foyer displayed photographs and quotes from the video along with a description of Ms. Mills' project. Additionally, CARD maintains a comprehensive website that includes information on PEPSA Partners and conference presentations, further expanding the possibility for the video to be seen internationally. A colleague at another school shared the video with practitioners in Malaysia as an example of ways inclusion can be practiced. In using video vignettes Ms. Mills had found dissemination methods that were easy to share, portable, crossed professional and language boundaries, and effectively shared her project through the heartfelt words and engagement of the children.

Engaging in the ARC process

Though Ms. Mills had not initially set out to engage in a research project, she quickly understood that is exactly what she was doing when she began to observe changes and realized the need to document. The pieces of the project fit naturally into the ARC. Formulating an inquiry on how best practice theory could be applied right away to the school setting reflects the first stage of the ARC, that of knowing what is hoped to be discovered and how it will fit into practice. The practitioner's university studies, conference and workshop attendance, and continual reading of professional journals informed the second stage of knowing about previous information. Asking questions of mentors and other teachers about how inclusion and collaborative relationships worked for them fit the third stage of the cycle.

Once the research cycle was recognized, informed consent from three different organizations was procured for all the students and adults involved in the project. Though the practitioner initially considered receiving consent from parents of the students as adequate, after more fully understanding this cycle she knew that she could have done a more thorough job of seeking fully informed consent from the students themselves. Gathering the information and making sense of it seemed an easy task initially through taking photographs and videos and telling others about her discoveries, but she needed a way to share the information that was brief, engaging, and in a portable format. How could she share the students' meaningful interactions and important social gains in a way that respectfully reflected the students' own impressions? She wanted to spread the news of her exciting discoveries to the winds to travel far and wide, with the hope that others would catch her enthusiasm. She wanted to make a lasting impact on those she was sharing with, so that they would be inspired to try collaboration and inclusion activities for themselves.

Sharing new information in new ways

There is no question that research-based practice is critical to student achievement. In the USA, the No Child Left Behind Act (2001) uses the phrase *scientifically based research* over 100 times when referring to educational practice. Despite an abundance of educational research, much of classroom practice does not reflect application of research, leaving proven instructional techniques waiting at the door (Forness, Kavale, Blum, & Lloyd, 1997, both cited in Landrum, Cook, Tankersley, & Fitzgerald, 2007). Informed, precise instruction is especially keen for students with disabilities who cannot recover from lack of educator knowledge as well as students without disabilities (Vaughn & Dammann, 2001, cited in Jones, 2009). Veteran teachers entrenched in their instructional routines may be even less likely to pursue and incorporate new strategies into their practice (Landrum et al., 2007). It seems particularly important for those respected and experienced in the field with leadership roles and who mentor novice teachers to be role models for using evidence-based methods to inform their teaching.

Traditional research practices convey information in ways that may not be easily accessible to practitioners, resulting in a gap between what researchers discover and what is put into practice in the classroom. Even though there is much research around educational outcomes, this has had minor impact on how teachers teach and what students actually learn (Viadero, 2009, cited in Smith, Richards-Tutor, & Cook, 2010). Accessibility, or ease of accessing and extracting information, can be difficult for practitioners even in widely researched areas. Teachers tasked to find research-based practices on reading instruction had great difficulty finding information that they could apply directly to practice. Perceived usability is another critical element of information presentation. If teachers can quickly see and understand how new techniques apply to their own teaching, they have more confidence and apply it more often. Researchers often assume their audience is mostly scholarly, making reports difficult to understand (Carnine, 1995b, cited in Carnine, 1997). Teachers may not even read professional journals and report a general mistrust of research because they often feel it is unrealistic to apply in the real-world classroom (Jones, 2009). Studies point to limited dissemination of research findings as one of the pertinent issues that must be addressed in order to close the research-to-practice gap (Bensimon, Polkinghorne, Bauman, & Vallejo, 2004, cited in Syed, Cortes, Osterhout, Morris, & Jones, 2009).

Though researchers exist on the cutting edge of discovery, they have maintained traditional modes of dissemination through professional avenues that often do not reach into the real-world classrooms meant to employ their discoveries. They have failed to tap new strategies to deliver critical information to users that are tailored in content and format (Lomas, 1997, cited in Ballew, Brownson, Haire-Joshu, Heath, & Kreuter, 2010). Rogers (2003, cited in Ballew et al., 2010) describes effective dissemination occurring in stages through the actions of researchers, the characteristics of practitioners, and the specific methods used for communicating information. Researchers can look to business models to overcome the current ineffective passive approach to dissemination, develop community partnerships, increase demand for evidence-based approaches, and create effective dissemination systems (Kreuter & Bernhardt, 2009; Bero, Grilli, Grimshaw, Harvey, Oxman, & Thompson, 1998, cited in Kreuter & Bernhardt, 2009). A marketing approach can improve how information is packaged and presented to be more enticing and easy to use. Through utilizing a variety of dissemination methods designed to meet the needs of the practitioner-consumer, information ends up being used where it is intended to improve instruction and raise student achievement.

Stage Seven of the Accessible Research Cycle: challenges to sharing discoveries

Research and teaching are more than professional endeavors, there is an art and a craft to both that require innovative thought and creative action processes. Dissemination can also be viewed as an art, to thoughtfully bridge research and practice in a way that is both teacher-friendly and aligns with teacher needs (Lomas, 1997, cited in Ballew et al., 2010; Carnine, 1997). Teachers want to hear about high-performing schools and classrooms, easily understand methodologies, and see how they can apply it right away in their own setting (Carnine, 1997). The experiences of teachers in classrooms and schools offers an insight into pedagogy that moves beyond research that tries to establish "proof" of a particular strategy (Jones, 2009; Smith et al., 2010). Indeed, information received from colleagues is rated significantly more useable than that read in journals (Cook & Cook, 2004, cited in Landrum et al., 2007). The use of "vividness" and compelling personal testimony may make research impacts seem more real and improve practitioner reactions (Foegen, Espin, Allinder, & Markell, 2001, cited in Landrum et al., 2007). Passionate and skilled researchers who share their knowledge in ways that are useable and accessible are more effective with dissemination (Bryson, Koegel, Koegel, Openden, Smith, & Nefdt, 2007).

A variety of active, multidirectional dissemination strategies encourage responsiveness to research (Masuda, Robinson, Elliott, & Eyles, 2009). Technology often already in place offers access to information in a variety of ways, including informational websites, webcasts, social networking, online learning communities, and video hosting sites. The National Center for Education Statistics (2000, cited in Jones, 2009) reported that 98% of schools had internet access in the year 2000. New teachers use the internet almost exclusively when searching for information to improve their practice (Jones, 2009). Internet technologies "represent a quite revolutionary way of managing and repurposing online information and knowledge repositories, including clinical and research information" (Boulos & Wheeler, 2007, cited in Lewis, Koston, Quartley, & Adsit, 2011, p. 155). Lewis et al. (2011) describe a community of practice comprised of individuals who share resources and collaborate around a common interest. This is a familiar framework for educators experienced with formal mentorships and informal information sharing. Using the internet as a format for communities of practice can further widen the scope of dissemination. The development of visual media lends itself to information casting, or visual dissemination of research information (Syed et al., 2009).

Returning to our example of Ms. Mills, she chose a video format to share her discoveries with colleagues, which met a need for the information to be accurate, accessible, and engaging. Though it seemed an ideal way to get other practitioners excited, her project was not without some problems. A SWOT analysis, commonly applied in business arenas to discover Strengths, Weaknesses, Opportunities, and Threats, was utilized to evaluate a webcast project of the 2009 Community College Futures Assembly, and serves as a good model with which to evaluate Ms. Mills video project as well (Syed et al., 2009).

- *Strengths:* Video provides accurate reporting (Bryson et al., 2007), as it does not rely on hearsay or what an observer might remember of an experience. The compact video camera was unobtrusive and very easy to use, with software on board for transfer to other media for editing purposes. Its size and hand-held use proved little to no distraction or discomfort to those being recorded, lending further accuracy in reporting. Since Ms. Mills had purchased the camera through previous year grant funds, there was very little associated cost. The resulting video information was very portable through the use of flash drives, compact disc storage, and video hosting websites that ease transmission of large data files. The media used to share information is small and easy to carry, simple to mail, and matches common computer input/output systems. The eight minutes of images, spoken messages, and music communicated the outcomes of the collaborative inclusion project in an engaging and meaningful way that impacted viewers beyond what words on paper could convey.
- *Weaknesses:* Despite being technically adequate with computers and having the ability to figure out most software and equipment issues, Ms. Mills

experienced difficulties with some areas of the video and sound editing. She had never created or edited a video, so initially she requested the assistance of a colleague at school to assist. The colleague had access to professional sound and video recording and editing, and agreed to help collect interviews from students and compile all the segments into the final video product. While he did assist with interview collection, the amount of time and effort to edit was underestimated, resulting in the colleague dropping out of the project. Ms. Mills learned "on the fly" to use a movie creation software program already on her computer. After many hours and mistakes, she finally had a product that was watchable, but clearly not professional. Reliance on other professionals necessitates commitment by all parties to carry through on their piece of the project for expected outcome of products.

- *Opportunities:* Multimedia presentation of research information is not commonly practiced, providing a rich and innovative resource for dissemination. Accessible technology allows for financially feasible methods of capturing and sharing information in multiple ways that meet the various needs of the practicing community. The video format promises fidelity in reporting of professional and peer discoveries, opening avenues for further exploration. Practitioner-researchers can shine a light on their previously sheltered discoveries, and can hope to gain a broad and diverse audience. Collaboration with researchers and other professionals can lead to formal study and potential publication, essentially sneaking in the back door of previously limiting academic journals. Once practitioners feel their opinions are valued, trust and readership of research-based practices improve, bringing more effective practice into the classroom.

- *Threats:* Considerations to information sharing through video production include commitment and relationships between team members, understanding of technology applications, and presentation in a format that is globally standardized. Producers must ensure that truly informed consent is inherent for all participants. Video content must reflect evidence that the approach is effective, must be respectful of all participants in language and impressions, and must describe the effects on all involved populations. Viewers should be able to clearly understand the approach and outcomes of the project (Carnine, 1997).

Though not without some problems, using a video to disseminate information worked well for Ms. Mills to share her story of collaboration, inclusion, and the positive effects it had on everyone involved. Better planning, application of research methodology from the inception of the project, and committed team members would nearly eliminate most of the issues. It was easy and even fun to capture the children's interactions and their honest feedback. Ms. Mills was very satisfied that the video showed what she intended, and sharing it with others and receiving positive feedback from parents and colleagues were personally and professionally rewarding. It was exciting and powerful to feel that she was positively influencing her students, other teachers, and the educational field. In addition to all her other hats she wore in life, she had a new one, that of practitioner-researcher.

Some final words on dissemination

Clearly, research stalls without appropriate dissemination, making effective information sharing a critical link between researchers and practitioners. New strategies for dissemination must consider the real world of teachers and the challenges they face with limited resources, more accountability, and increasingly diverse learners. De-mystification of the research process through more accessible and useable information can lead to better classroom practice and achievement for students. Additionally, practitioners may begin to see themselves as part of the research process, may more formally investigate new inquiries for study, and share their findings with colleagues in ways that are engaging and instantly applicable.

References

Ballew, P., Brownson, R.C., Haire-Joshu, D., Heath, G.W., & Kreuter, M.W. (2010). Dissemination of effective physical activity interventions: Are we applying the evidence? *Health Education Research, 25*(2), 185–198. Doi: 10.1093/her/cyq003.

Bellini, S. (2006). *Building social relationships.* Shawnee Mission, KS: Autism Asperger Publishing Co.

Bryson, S.E., Koegel, L.K., Koegel, R.L., Openden, D., Smith, I.M., & Nefdt, N. (2007). Large scale dissemination and community implementation of pivotal response treatment: Program description and preliminary data. *Research & Practice for Persons with Severe Disabilities, 32*(2), 142–153. Available at: http://www.atypon-link.com.ezproxy.lib.usf.edu/TASH/doi/pdf/10.5555/rpsd.32.2.142?cookieSet=1.

Carnine, D. (1997). Bridging the research-to-practice gap. *Exceptional Children, 63*(4), 513–521. Available at : http://find.galegroup.com.ezproxy.lib.usf.edu/gtx/infomark. do?&contentSet=IAC-Documents&type=retrieve&tabID=T002&prodId=ITOF&docI d=A19616678&source=gale&srcprod=ITOF&userGroupName=tamp59176&version =1.0.

Friese, B., & Bogenschneider, K. (2009). The voice of experience: How social scientists communicate family research to policymakers. *Family Relations, 58*(2), 229–243. Doi: 10.1111/j.1741-3729.2008.00549.x.

Jones, M.L. (2009). A study of novice Special Educators' views of evidence-based practices. *Teacher Education and Special Education: The Journal of the Teacher Education Division of the Council for Exceptional Children, 32*(2), 101–120. Doi: 10.1177/0888406409333777.

Kreuter, M.W., & Bernhardt, J.M. (2009). Reframing the dissemination challenge: A marketing and distribution perspective. *American Journal of Public Health, 99*(2), 2123–2127. Doi: 10.2105/AJPH.2008.155218.

Landrum, T.J., Cook, B.G., Tankersley, M., & Fitzgerald, S. (2007). Teacher perceptions of the useability of intervention information from personal versus data-based sources. *Education and Treatment of Children, 30*(4), 27–42. Doi: 10.1353/etc.2007.0025.

Lewis, L.A., Koston, Z., Quartley, M., & Adsit, J. (2011). Virtual communities of practice: Bridging research and practice using Web 2.0. *Journal of Educational Technology Systems*, *39*(2), 155–161. Doi. 10.2190/ET.39.2.e.

Masuda J.R., Robinson, K., Elliott, S., & Eyles, J. (2009). Disseminating chronic disease prevention "to or with" Canadian public health systems. *Health Education & Behavior*, *36*(6), 1026–1050. Doi: 10.1177/1090198109339276.

Mawhinney, L. (2009). Let's lunch and learn: Professional knowledge sharing in teachers' lounges and other congregational spaces. *Teaching and Teacher Education*, *26*(4), 972–978. Doi: 10.1016/i.tate.2009.10.039.

Smith, G.J., Richards-Tutor, C., & Cook, B.G. (2010). Using teacher narratives in the dissemination of research-based practices. *Intervention in School and Clinic*, *46*(2), 67–70. Doi: 10.1177/1053451210375301.

Syed, S., Cortes, J., Osterhout, J., Morris, P.A., & Jones, E. (2009). Webcasting the 2009 Community College Futures Assembly: Making emergent knowledge accessible in practice. *Community College Journal of Research & Practice*, *33*(11), 855–865. Doi: 10.1080/10668920903167634.

Legislation

No Child Left Behind Act of 2001, 20 U.S.C., 6301 (2001).

Chapter 9

Relating discoveries to practice
Student self-monitoring

Aisha Holmes

It is another Friday afternoon. As I reflect on my classroom instruction for this week, I feel frustrated. I focus on one student in particular. I begin to ask questions about how to provide a meaningful inclusive experience where he has full access to the curriculum. Currently, he exhibits off-task behavior (calling out) that interrupts the flow of classroom instruction and each student's learning experience. How can I help this student decrease off-task behaviors that disrupt the flow of classroom instruction? I decide to engage in an action research project to evaluate the use of a contingency-based self-management tool to evaluate the effects on off-task (calling out) behavior with this particular student.

Introduction

Relating discoveries to practice can be a challenging task. In the above scenario, the practitioner decides to implement an action research project to evaluate the use of a strategy to promote a meaningful inclusive experience for one student. The goal is to relate the outcome of the action research project to continued classroom practice. The practitioner may consider the following questions throughout the process of the action research project:

- How do the findings of this project inform my professional practice?
- How do the findings in this project inform the professional practice of others?
- How do the findings increase my understanding of children's responses?

This chapter considers the importance of embedding research findings into practice and describes how an action research project designed around the seventh stage of the Accessible Research Cycle (ARC) impacted the teaching and learning of an 8th grade classroom in southwest Florida. It will share how discoveries made in the course of conducting the action research project related back to practice in the classroom. The chapter will provide a discussion of the motivation that led to the teacher's engagement in the inquiry process, and the applications of the outcomes from a contingency-based self-monitoring strategy to support one student's ownership of behavior and learning. Furthermore, the chapter will highlight how the findings informed professional practice of the practitioner and of others in the school, and how the process of inquiry increased professionals' understandings of the student's responses. At the end of this chapter, practitioners will be better informed in relating discoveries to practice.

The context

This project occurred in a public middle school in southwest Florida in the United States where a practitioner named Norinda developed an action research project for one 8th grade student named Gavin with a disability label of specific learning disability (SLD). Gavin received his label during his second year in 3rd grade. He was retained after his first year in third grade because he did not pass the state standardized assessment and did not respond to specific academic interventions. Gavin continued 4th and 5th grades, ages 10–12, in general education classrooms with the support of a paraprofessional. When Gavin transitioned to middle school, he began to exhibit a greater need for increased individualized academic support, which was provided in the self-contained classroom.

Gavin was chosen for this action research project because he displayed a substantial amount of off-task (calling out) behavior that disrupted the learning environment. He was in a self-contained classroom of 8th grade students, typically ages 13–14, alongside 13 other students. The classroom had one special education teacher and one paraprofessional. He attended each class with the same group of students and paraprofessional for all core subjects and one exploratory class (reading, language arts, social studies, science, math, and 2-D art). The school followed a special education provision model that included three classroom settings where students received access to the general education curriculum: self-contained, resource, and regular. The self-contained classroom included students with a range of disabilities, a special educator and paraprofessional for all four core subjects (language arts, math, science, social studies). The resource classroom included students with a range of disabilities and a special educator for math and/or reading only. The general classroom included students with and without disabilities and a general educator where students with disabilities receive accommodations to support individual needs. Accommodations may include academic, behavior, and physical supports that allow for greater access of instructional materials and interaction with peers and the environment.

Little (2005) conducted a survey of 154 teachers to determine the most troublesome behaviors practitioners in secondary schools encounter. The results indicated that talking out of turn and hindering other children were the most problematic behaviors in the classroom. These minor violations of classroom rules affect the learning of the child exhibiting the behavior and also disrupt peer success. Norinda was concerned with the amount of off-task behavior, in this case calling out, that one student displayed in the classroom. The student called-out during group and independent activities. The vignette above closely resembled Norinda's classroom experience, which prompted her to engage in the ARC.

The challenge

Norinda's project focused on improving behavior and learning outcomes for her student by decreasing off-task behavior and as such she was concerned with stage seven of the ARC, which considers "how discoveries relate to practice." Norinda needed a strategy to link research to practice and she was able to reflect on the findings that emerged from research applying what she learned to enhance her practice (Schoen & Nolen, 2004). When conducting investigations, practitioners face the challenge of implementing effective action research projects in the classroom. To make beneficial changes in the classroom, practitioners need a concise understanding of what the issue is they are trying to address and why. The ARC provides practitioners with a structure to guide action research projects and to consider the implementation of the outcomes of that research.

What did the practitioner want to know?

The first step in action research is to identify what academic and/or behavior tasks need to change. Norinda wanted to know if the use of contingency-based self-monitoring would decrease off-task behaviors that disrupt the flow of the classroom. With increased accountability measures and the call for implementation of evidence-based strategies, the practitioner decided to conduct an action research project focused on improved student behavior outcome.

Empowering students using contingency-based self-management

Costa and Kallick (2004) define the characteristics of self-directed learners. Self-directed learners are able to exhibit the dispositions and habits of mind required to self-manage, self-monitor, and self-modify when confronted with complex and ambiguous intellectually demanding tasks. People who employ self-management are able to control their first impulse for action and delay premature conclusions. People who employ self-monitoring are able to think about their own thinking, behaviors, biases, and beliefs as well as about the effect such processes and states of mind have on others and on the environment. People who are self-modifying can change themselves through reflecting on their own experiences while evaluating, analyzing, and constructing meaning. Self-managing, self-monitoring, and self-modifying functions can transfer across subject areas and distinguish peak performers in all walks of life. It is crucial that students with disabilities are supported in the development of self-management procedures to support meaningful inclusion and access to the general education curriculum.

Self-monitoring improves attention, academic productivity, and decreases off-task behavior in the classroom (Amato-Zech, Hoff, & Doepke, 2006). Self-monitoring includes two processes: self-recording and self-observation. Self-observation requires students to notice a specific behavior and recognize when the behavior being monitored has occurred. Self-monitoring can decrease the need for external agents such as teachers, paraprofessionals, and peers to enforce behavior management techniques. The use of self-monitoring techniques can promote behavior change in untrained settings.

Contingency-based self-management is an educational technique that allows students to track their own behavior (self-monitoring) while receiving tangible reinforcers (self-reward) to promote success (Hallahan & Kauffman, 2006; Reid, Trout & Schartz, 2005). Contingency-based self-management uses a written contingency-based contract developed by the practitioner and student. The contract is signed and implemented only after the student understands its purpose and the expectations. The practitioner in this action research project chose this strategy with the student to encourage active engagement. The practitioner felt this student would benefit as an active participant in tracking his own off-task behavior, which would increase awareness of his actions, leading to decreased off-task behavior. Increased awareness of actions provides students an ongoing opportunity to engage in the inclusive classroom. When students understand their actions impact the learning environment, they are more likely to meaningfully engage in the inclusive classroom.

Polloway, Patton, and Serna (2005) suggest the contingency-based contract must include clear terms, be fair, honest, positive and age-appropriate, meet the student's needs, and be used systematically. The use of contingency contracts increases motivation for students to follow through with expectations and tasks using external control. Self-monitoring is one component of self-management. Self-management represents intrinsic control, as the student becomes more conscious of his or her own thinking processes and task approach strategies (Reeve, 1990). Self-monitoring, or recording, requires the target behavior to be defined, the identification of functional reinforcer(s), the self-monitoring tool to be designed, the student to be taught the proper use of the tool, and how to fade the use of the device. Fading the use of the self-monitoring tool promotes maintenance and generalization. Successful use of self-monitoring should promote maintenance of acquired behaviors and skills over time and ultimately generalize to other settings and other behaviors (Polloway, Patton, & Serna, 2005).

The use of self-monitoring can take many shapes as strategies vary and change, according to student needs. For example, a self-monitoring strategy that can be employed in the classroom would be to give a student a timer to check progress on an assignment every five minutes to minimize non-engaged time. Self-monitoring techniques should take minimal time and effort to use and help the learner progress toward a specific goal. Norinda decided to use a strategy that matched Gavin's needs and was meaningful to him.

Data collection

This practitioner inquiry project focused on an individual student. In the literature this is usually referred to as single-case design. Norinda decided to use a mixed methods approach to her inquiry because this method promotes reflective inquiry and critical analysis of the student's progress. Mixed methods use numerical data to add meaning to narratives specific to the process and outcome of the research inquiry. Norinda collected both quantitative data (record of off-task behavior) and qualitative data (daily practitioner–student conference) in order to produce a more complete picture of the student's progress. Gavin's initial assessment data was collected using a basic tally system to determine the occurrences of off-task behavior during a specific time period, one week across five classes— reading, language arts, math, science, and social studies. This initial assessment served as a baseline that would later be used to determine if the implementation of contingency-based self-monitoring decreased Gavin's off-task behavior of calling-out. During the initial data collection Gavin displayed the off-task behavior of calling out more than 30 times per day across five class periods. Norinda decided to develop a self-monitoring contract the student could use to self-track his progress (Figure 9.1).

Before the start of the practitioner inquiry project Gavin received training on the process of self-monitoring and use of the contingency contract. He did not receive explicit guidance or help from his exploratory class teacher and paraprofessional, they were simply aware of what was going on. The frequency of the target behavior (calling out) was recorded with the goal of decreasing off-task behavior over the four weeks of the action research project. Norinda and Gavin negotiated an acceptable frequency of the target behavior for each week. Norinda and Gavin's goal was to decrease the target behavior by 50% at the end of the four-week period. They set the following goals: week one: no more than five occurrences of off-task behavior (calling out) during each class period; week four: no more than two occurrences of off-task behavior (calling out) during each class period.

Gavin determined his contingency would be 20 minutes of computer time during homeroom if he met his goal, and lunch detention if he did not meet his goal. Students are more motivated to complete tasks when they are able to set personal goals and have an opportunity to address frustration to avoid anxiety (CAST, 2011). He recorded each time he called out in class using a simple tally system. To discuss goal attainment, Norinda and Gavin met for the last 10 minutes of the day. Norinda recorded notes on their conversations and used the information to help Gavin plan toward success. Naturally, Gavin may have forgotten to record occurrences of off-task behavior, especially in the beginning of the project. During the 10-minute daily meeting, Norinda and Gavin would

Self-monitoring contract

Student name: _____ Week of: _____

Student signature: _____ Teacher signature: _____

Target behavior: off-task, calling out during class at any time

Goal: 5 or less occurrences of target behavior each class period

Consequences

Goal met: 15 minutes of computer time T-time (homeroom) daily

Goal not met: lunch detention daily (sit away from peers in the café)

Directions: Place one tally at the appropriate day and period when target behavior occurs.

	Period 1	Period 2	Period 3	Period 4	Period 5	Period 6
Monday						
Tuesday						
Wednesday						
Thursday						
Friday						

Figure 9.1 Self-monitoring contract

evaluate his level of engagement and discuss occurrences where he might have forgotten to record off-task behavior and how this could affect the results of the contingency-based self-monitoring process. Gavin was vigilant in recording his off-task behaviors as he expressed delight in the success of achieving his goals.

How do discoveries relate to practice?

The findings of the practitioner inquiry project were significant for several reasons. First, Norinda learned that engagement in the action research process was not as time-consuming as she had anticipated. Second, she learned that students benefit from contingency-based self-management, thus relieving some of the control she felt was necessary in governing student behavior. Finally, she learned that incorporating contingency-based self-management in the classroom increased student motivation and self-determination.

At the start of the practitioner inquiry project, Norinda was hesitant to begin. She felt overwhelmed by the thought of committing time to learn about the action research process and effective classroom management strategies. She became increasingly concerned when she realized she would have to dedicate time to teaching Gavin how to use the contingency-based self-management tool and then meet 10 minutes per day to discuss goal attainment. What Norinda realized within the first few days was that she actually committed less time dealing with Gavin's off-task behavior of calling out in the classroom. For example, when Gavin called out and disrupted the flow of learning it would often take Norinda a few minutes to get him and the rest of the class back on task and focused. As Gavin called out less in the classroom, Norinda found that the students were able to maintain longer durations of active engagement in the classroom. Gavin's 2-D art teacher reported similar findings.

Norinda realized it was important to relinquish some control over Gavin's off-task behaviors. If students with disabilities do not have an opportunity to engage in self-monitoring strategies, then other people (e.g., practitioner, peers) may control tasks the student could do for him/herself (Agran, King-Sears, Wehmeyer, & Copeland, 2003). Norinda had become accustomed to directing all of her students most of the day, in even most basic tasks (e.g., grant students permission to move about the classroom to gather materials to complete assigned tasks). At the close of the practitioner inquiry project Norinda recognized the positive changes Gavin had made and she chose to relinquish control in other aspects of her classroom management repertoire.

Norinda noticed a change in Gavin's overall attitude toward active engagement in the classroom. Gavin reported that he felt important because people listened to him and believed in him and he felt confident that his need (to decrease off-task behavior) was being met while receiving appropriate consequences. Norinda was surprised to hear that Gavin did not initially know how often he called out during class and he was anxious to decrease the behavior. He was proud of his successes and disappointed with his shortcomings, which was motivation for him to use the contract seriously and tirelessly. Wehmeyer (1996, p. 42) defined self-determination as "acting as the primary causal agent in one's life and making choices and decisions regarding one's quality of life free from undue external influence or interference." Gavin was able to engage in a self-management process that promoted choice-making while he also learned that it is sometimes necessary to use external factors such as contingency-based self-monitoring contracts to help reach behavior goals.

How do the findings in this project inform the professional practice of others?

It is important practitioners share their findings with others. Norinda wanted to share her findings with other educators as she believed they could also benefit from the use of contingency-based self-management tools to address off-task behaviors in the classroom. She was also interested in receiving feedback about the process and outcomes of the action research project. Norinda was able to present her findings during a grade-level professional collaborative learning meeting that included all 8th grade teachers and the school's principal, assistant principal, behavior specialist, and guidance counselor.

Based on the success of the practitioner inquiry project in Norinda's class and across campus with Gavin, the 8th grade teachers decided to implement similar contingency-based self-management strategies across campus with students that exhibited various off-task behaviors in the classroom. Lan (2005) suggests one way to promote self-monitoring is to introduce students to self-monitoring strategies their peers have used successfully. The practitioners appreciated the simplicity of the contingency-based self-management contract and were anxious to use the strategy with their students. The practitioners who adopted the strategy reconvened in six weeks and reported that the use of contingency-based self-management strategies had improved student behavior and learning. The administrators then decided to include individual contingency-based self-monitoring school-wide.

How do the findings increase my understanding of children's responses?

As Norinda completed the practitioner inquiry project, she realized Gavin was more capable at monitoring his own behaviors than she could. It was necessary for her to release some external control in regulating Gavin's off-task behavior. Because some students have difficulty self-regulating their behavior, explicit instruction may be necessary (CAST, 2011). The use of contingency-based self-management provided Gavin with an opportunity to increase self-regulation, connect to the external environment, and support his intrinsic abilities to connect with his needs as a learner. Norinda was able to promote meaningful inclusion in the classroom and greater access to the general education curriculum by supporting Gavin's desire to decrease his off-task behavior.

Practitioners should be encouraged to make informed decisions before implementing procedures, plans of action, etc. to support the needs of their students. Hallahan and Kauffman (2006) suggest that as the students' on-task behavior increases, academic productivity will also increase. Norinda discovered that Gavin's grades improved across class settings as his level of active engagement in the classroom increased. Norinda began the practitioner inquiry project concerned about the time commitment required. She realized that she spent less time addressing Gavin's off-task behaviors, therefore minimizing overall class disruptions.

Emerging issues

Practitioners may encounter issues while engaged in the ARC. Norinda discovered students were reluctant to participate in the practitioner inquiry project. Norinda initially wanted to engage four students in the project who displayed varying off-task behaviors in her class of 14, but through the informed consent process only one student and family agreed to participate. When asked if they would like to participate, some of the students shared their feelings that the project would be boring, would take up too much time, they didn't need any help with behaviors, and others. Norinda found that some of the students who exhibited off-task behaviors were not interested in changing their behaviors to improve their academic success and decrease class disruptions. Although she sent home letters to the parents about the action research project, she received minimal feedback. Norinda also made a commitment to meet with Gavin for the last 10 minutes of the school day to discuss progress and clarify any questions and concerns of the student. It was important Norinda and Gavin remembered to meet at the end of the day. Norinda posted a reminder message on her desk while Gavin used a watch with an alarm or the wall clock in the classroom to remind them both to meet at the end of the day. It is important practitioners address issues as they arise during the practitioner inquiry project to determine what adjustments need to be made to ensure success.

Conclusion

Presented in this chapter is an example of how one practitioner-researcher engaged in the ARC in order to relate discoveries to practice. As a result of engaging in the ARC, the practitioner discovered that contingency-based self-monitoring was an effective behavior management strategy that provided her student an opportunity to effectively self-manage his behavior. Engagement in the ARC helped the practitioner navigate the process of developing a sound practitioner inquiry project. She was able to share how the use of contingency-based self-monitoring supported the needs of one student, thus encouraging other practitioners and administrators to use similar self-management tools across the school campus. The findings of the study changed the practitioner's perception of her student's ability to self-manage his own behavior, thus decreasing the need to maintain full control over her students' actions.

References

Agran, M., King-Sears, M., Wehmeyer, M., & Copeland, S. (2003). *Teachers guides to inclusive practices: Student-directed learning.* Baltimore, MD: Brookes Publishing Co.

Amato-Zech, N., Hoff, K., & Doepke, K. (2006). Increasing on-task behavior in the classroom: Extension of self-monitoring strategies. *Psychology in the Schools, 43*(2), 211–221.

CAST (2011). *Universal design for learning guidelines, version 2.0.* Wakefield, MA: Author.

Costa, A., & Kallick, B. (2004). Launching self-directed learners. *Educational Leadership, 62*(1), 51–55.

Hallahan, D., & Kauffman, J. (2006). *Exceptional learners: Introduction to special education* (10th ed.). Boston, MA: Pearson Education, Inc.

Lan, W. (2005). Self-monitoring and its relationship with educational level and task importance. *Educational Psychology, 25*(1), 109–127.

Little, E. (2005). Secondary school teachers' perceptions of students' problem behaviours. *Educational Psychology, 25*(4), 369–377.

Polloway, E.A., Patton, J.R., & Serna, L. (2005). *Strategies for teaching learners with special needs* (8th ed.). Upper Saddle River, NJ: Merrill/Prentice Hall.

Reeve, R.E. (1990). ADHD: Facts and fallacies. In E.A. Polloway, J.R. Patton, & L. Serna (2005), *Strategies for teaching learners with special needs* (8th ed.). Upper Saddle River, NJ: Merrill/Prentice Hall.

Reid, R., Trout, A.L., & Schartz, M. (2005). Self-regulation interventions for children with attention deficit/hyperactivity disorder. *Exceptional Children, 71*, 361–377.

Schoen, S.F., & Nolen, J. (2004). Action research: Decreasing acting out behavior and increasing learning. *Teaching Exceptional Children, 37*(1), 26–29.

Wehmeyer, M.L. (1996). Self-determination as an educational outcome: Why is it important to children, youth, and adults with disabilities? In P. Wehman (Ed.), *Life beyond the classroom: Transition strategies for young people with disabilities* (pp. 42–43). Baltimore, MD: Paul H. Brookes.

Chapter 10

The ARC in action

Practitioners' perspectives

Phyllis Jones, Teresa Whitehurst and Jo Egerton

Introduction

The ARC was developed as an international initiative between the leadership and research staff at a residential special school in the UK and an associate professor of special education at the University of South Florida, USA. In trialing the design, it was field tested by 49 special education practitioners in New Zealand. This chapter offers an insight into their perspectives on the ARC, which was introduced as part of a ten-day intensive professional development workshop focused upon 'Inquiry into teaching'.

The participants

The self-selected participant group was made up of principals, assistant principals, classroom teachers, speech and language therapists, physiotherapists and occupational therapists working in special educational settings. These settings included special schools and special satellite classrooms located on mainstream school sites. Table 10.1 shows the professional range of workshop participants, the majority of which were classroom teachers.

Table 10.1 Professions of the course participants

Profession	Number in workshop (n = 49)
Teacher	27
Principal or Assistant Principal	10
Speech and Language Therapist	5
Occupational Therapist	4
Physiotherapist	3

Informed consent

At the beginning of the workshop, course participants were informed about how the ARC had developed, its role in the current training and the intention to gather their views about it to improve understanding of practitioner inquiry. They were told that the data would be collected as part of a customary end-of-workshop evaluation survey. It was explained how the data would be managed, analysed and shared with others. All 49 participants attending the workshops completed the survey and all signed an informed consent sheet.

The workshop

The extended workshop included an introduction to research in special education. It aimed to present a research process that was accessible and that school-based professionals could relate to their own practice. The workshop presented:

- an introduction to inquiry-based practices;
- shared case studies demonstrating a range of school-based action research projects;
- interactive workshop sessions where participants had an opportunity to plan their own research projects collaboratively based on the ARC.

Collecting perceptions of the ARC

Participants' feedback about the ARC was collected as part of a customary work-shop evaluation survey. The survey included two types of questions about the ARC:

1 *Closed questions*: Participants were asked to use a Likert scale to rate the potential of the ARC as a tool to support practice in a special educational setting (e.g. for potential usefulness of the ARC to practice, 1 represented 'no use' and 10 represented 'very useful').
2 *Open questions* encouraged practitioners to share their descriptions of how they might use the ARC to engage in school-based inquiry.

Data management and analysis

Responses to the Likert scale questions were analysed using simple count frequency and collated in a table format. Four researchers, working independently to increase internal validity (Mays & Pope, 1995), coded individual statements within the responses to open questions by emergent themes. Collaborative discussion between the researchers led to agreement on four over-arching emergent themes. Once the four themes were identified, the four researchers, again working separately, allocated each statement to one of the four themes.

Results and emerging themes

Responses to closed questions

Figures 10.1 and 10.2 present the collated responses to the two closed questions that focused upon the level of perceived usefulness and usability of the ARC.

Of the 49 practitioners who completed the survey, 38% gave the ARC a usefulness rating of 10 on the Likert scale, with a further 47% giving a rating of either 8 or 9, suggesting a perception of useful to very useful for the ARC. None of the participants rated the ARC's usefulness below point 5 on the scale.

Of the 49 practitioners surveyed, 28% felt the ARC would be 'very easy' to use (giving a score of 10) while a further 45% gave a score of either 8 or 9 on the Likert scale, suggesting a perception of easy to very easy for use of the ARC. Again, none of the participants gave a score below 5 (quite easy).

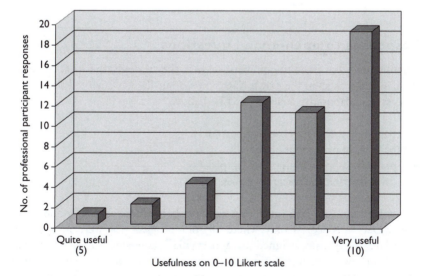

Figure 10.1 Practitioner ratings of the usefulness of the ARC as a tool within a special education setting

Note: n = 49.

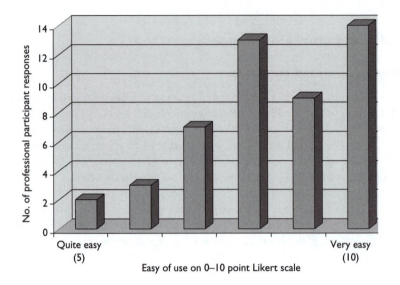

Figure 10.2 Practitioner ratings of the ease of use of the ARC in a special educational setting

Note: 1 = 'not at all easy'; 10 = 'very easy' (n = 49).

Responses to open-ended questions

Practitioners were asked to comment on how they thought the ARC could help them as researchers in their own classrooms. Four themes emerged through the process of collaborative analysis described above:

- confidence in themselves as researchers;
- benefits of practitioner research;
- practical support in the research process;
- de-mystifying the research process.

In total, there were 126 qualitative statements made by the workshop participants. Data was scored only where all four professionals were in agreement regarding the theme assigned to a particular statement. Of the 126 statements, 110 were unanimously coded for a particular theme. The remaining 16 statements were coded differently by the individual researchers and so were discounted from the data analysis. The data outcomes are presented in Table 10.2.

Table 10.2 Number of statements assigned to emergent themes

Theme	Number of unanimous statement allocations (n = 110)
Benefits from practitioner research	52
Practical support in the research process	37
De-mystifying the research process	17
Confidence in themselves as practitioners	4

Emergent themes

The theme with the highest number of practitioner statements (n = 52) allocated to it was 'Benefits from practitioner research'. This theme included practitioners' ideas for meaningful research projects identified with the support of the ARC. Practitioners perceived that the ARC supported them to: 'share information', 'improve teaching practice', 'focus on areas of doubt or concern to explore solutions', and 'validate school practices in a structured way'. These responses support findings from other research that structured inquiry into practice in school has the potential to improve practice, support problem solving and support solution generation (Ponte, Ax, Beijaard, & Wubbels, 2004; Rinaldo, 2005; Roberts, 1993).

The second most frequently assigned theme reflects the theory of Rinaldo (2005): that the ARC offers practical support in the research process. One teacher commented that '[It] opens the way for me to approach my school and get the Practitioner Research Cycle in place – something I've been thinking but not saying.'

Other responses showed practitioner perceptions of the practical nature of the ARC, and how it was 'logical', and 'cyclical – you can see the beginning and the end'. One respondent stated that '[It] guides you systematically through the various stages of inquiry.' This showed that practitioners felt that research, as expressed through the ARC, had the potential to provide a way to systematically conduct research into classroom and school practices. This resonates with conceptions of the relationship between research and practice as cyclical and flowing (Christenson, Slutsky, Bendau, Covert, Dyer, Risko, & Johnston, 2002; Reis-Jorge, 2007).

A further theme that emerged from practitioners' survey statements related to how the ARC de-mystified the research process for them. This is exemplified by one respondent who commented that '[The ARC] used everyday language to engage all staff, parents, etc., whilst making the whole process seem simple and user friendly.'

Connecting everyone in the school to the process of inquiry is important. Christenson et al. (2002) analysed practitioners' views of a more traditional research process and reported that fears were focused upon traditional methodologies and language. The responses from the practitioners in New Zealand support the view that the ARC may offer a positive contribution to overcoming the fears highlighted in Christenson's research.

Finally, four statements made by respondents suggested that, for some, the ARC led to 'confidence in themselves as researchers'. Initially, this was thought to be a discrete theme in its own right. However, while the theme of confidence may be obvious from some practitioner statements, in others, the theme was underlying factors that sat more readily in other themes. In this way, confidence to begin a project of inquiry can be seen as a complex phenomena influenced by many factors. However, one participant shared the importance of the ARC in giving them the confidence to begin the process of inquiry: '[The ARC] serves as an encouragement to attempt research in the classroom.' This supports the established view that practitioner research can increase the self-confidence of teachers, which in turn can affect change within the school or classroom settings (Reis-Jorge, 2007).

Conclusion

This chapter has offered an insight into the perceptions of a group of 49 New Zealand special education practitioners about the ARC when it was presented to them as part of an extended workshop on inquiry into classroom practices. Educators have long been eager to participate in professional investigative inquiry, but dissuaded from doing so by conceptions of traditional educational research methodologies. These practitioners found that the ARC facilitated meaningful and accessible inquiry into practice. Creating a research-informed profession empowers practitioners to become agents of change. While the experiences of this small participant group cannot be generalised, we hope that the ARC can support others like them to become reflective, strategic, investigative, inquiring practitioners. The New Zealand practitioners found that the framework of support offered by the ARC was a helpful scaffold to practice-based inquiry and ensured that attention was paid to creating higher levels of rigor and validity. It seemed, within this research, that one of the overarching positive contributions of the ARC was a shared understandable language of school-based inquiry, which bridged what might have previously been perceived as an insurmountable barrier between the worlds of schooling and research (Saunders, 2007). The ARC supports practitioners to become producers of knowledge – knowledge that we hope can contribute to shared understandings and developments of school practice. In doing this, the role of the practitioner as a producer of research is both valuable and valued, and the role of the educator as both teacher and researcher is validated.

References

Christenson, M., Slutsky, R., Bendau, S., Covert, J., Dyer, J., Risko, G., & Johnston, M. (2002). The rocky road of teachers becoming action researchers. *Teaching and Teacher Education, 18,* 259–272.

Mays, N., & Pope, C. (1995). Rigour and qualitative research. *British Medical Journal, 311,* 109–112.

Ponte, P., Ax, J., Beijaard, D., & Wubbels, T. (2004). Teachers' development of professional knowledge through action research and the facilitation of this by teacher educators. *Teaching and Teacher Education, 20,* 571–588.

Reis-Jorge, J. (2007). Teachers' conceptions of teacher-research and self-perceptions as enquiring practitioners – a longitudinal case study. *Teaching and Teacher Education, 23,* 402–417.

Rinaldo, V. (2005). Today's practitioner is both qualitative and quantitative researcher. *High School Journal, 89*(1), 72–77.

Roberts, J.R. (1993). Evaluating the impacts of teacher research. *System, 21*(1), 1–19.

Saunders, L. (2007). Professional values and research values: from dilemmas to diversity. In A. Campbell and S. Groundwater-Smith (Eds.) *An ethical approach to practitioner research.* London: Routledge.

Chapter 11

Back to the future

Moving forward with practitioner research

Ann Fergusson

Introduction

This chapter seeks to complete the journey of this book by drawing on stories of practitioner research from the past. Not to take a historical perspective, but to see the historical context as a valuable and constructive place from which to look forward to plan the next steps of the research journey. There is much to be learnt from reflecting on how a strong relationship between research and practice in education is being forged – not only in terms of the impact and outcomes but, as importantly, also in the process by which these gains have been made and the foundations of new learning and knowledge within the field laid down. Indeed, Foreman-Peck (2005, p. 36) warns that:

> [T]eachers cannot ignore research because, whether they approve of it or not, it enters into their professional lives. Not only do they need to be aware of research, they need to know how it can be used.

That view could be taken a step further to suggest it can be of even greater value when they undertake that research themselves and, importantly, when in collaboration with professional or experienced researchers. The Accessible Research Cycle (ARC), as shown by the work of the practitioner researchers in the previous chapters, is one way by which professional researchers and practitioners can open and sustain a dialogue about research in schools and build shared expectations.

What's useful from school-based research?

Some educational research and development stories from the relatively new field of special education illustrate how principles and practice have moved from a broad focus on training or care towards one of education for all, enabled by creative personalised and differentiated approaches.

The 1970s saw the growth of a host of very diverse, and often contradictory, practice as this new student group joined the school population following the

Education for All Handicapped Children Act (1975) in the USA and, in the UK, the Education (Handicapped Children) Act 1970. Schools independently selected their approaches – from the very experiential and experimental sensory bombardment, introduced as a direct contrast to the previous passive and often under-stimulated experiences, to the sometimes extreme control of, for example, precision teaching (Lindsley, 1968) and behaviour modification (Ullmann and Krasner, 1965); others focused on addressing the delayed developmental progress of students which became the 'curriculum'.

Educational settings began to reflect professionally on the haphazard nature of this stance, and to move towards more considered strategies, some adopting a more systematic researching approach. This was a positive catalyst to developing more innovative and appropriate curricula, approaches to enabling learners, and the essential resources to support this learning for students with special educational needs. Many such developments, now considered established mainstream and common practice, were initiated and pioneered through the personal action research endeavours of individual practitioners in their own unique school settings. For example, work on sensory approaches and multisensory environments was originally developed as an advanced diploma thesis by Flo Longhorn, later published in 1988; early work by practitioners on the use of rebus symbols to support language and literacy began with Jones (1972) and van Oosterom and Devereux (1982); while McBrien and Weightman (1980) investigated techniques of room management and staff deployment. Intensive Interaction (for example, Hewett, 1986; Nind and Hewett, 1988; Hewett and Nind, 1989; Barber, 2011) which is now an internationally accepted way of working to value and promote the communicative exchange of people with learning disabilities, had its origins with a group of teachers working with people with learning disabilities in the school of a long-stay hospital where they worked.

The different ways in which researchers and practitioners have historically approached inquiry is the basis of the distance between them, but this may also be true of different groups of practitioners with the same aim in mind but working from different perspectives. In the examples below of working with Intensive Interaction, two groups of teachers took parallel journeys of discovery. The first group, working in a long-stay hospital, based their research strategies for working with their students on a classical research perspective involving a thorough review of the literature on very established theories of early mother–infant dyads and had developed some systematic processes to document and reflect upon their findings for this different population of young people with learning disabilities.

As a practitioner at that same time, the author recalls that she and her school colleagues were working along very similar lines, striving for the same purposes of meaningfully reaching and communicating with 'hard to reach' students. Together, as a group of inquirers, they had not employed the same rigour in their 'researching'; in fact, they certainly did not even view their explorations as research. They worked at a more intuitive level, using a curriculum development approach, following their professional hunches and informally sharing their findings and interpretations with each other at the end of a school day. They did keep copious records of their findings, using over-complicated schedules that hindered and clouded ideas and outcomes. However, reading less comprehensively with a focus on psychology, they had not discovered the same literature on the topic, or the insights of the Nind and Hewett team, which would have helped to make sense of their data and suggest potential next steps for progress. What did make a difference to the group's non-systematic 'researching' was a conference event sharing ideas and practice on 'Interactive Approaches'. All was revealed! Hearing the fruits of the research carried out by Nind and Hewett provided their missing puzzle pieces. This emphasised the value of employing an action research approach as a structure or framework to guide and focus their developments and innovations with more rigorous methods (Hewett and Nind, 1988). From that point, they returned to school with research 'tools' that enabled them to develop a clearer vision and understanding, which in turn led to improved interactions with their own students. When innovating, professional knowledge and experience combined with enthusiasm and determination are never going to be as effective as research. The key difference to success is the systematic structure and cycle employed through a research perspective – the 'Identification–Plan–Do–Review' cycle. The support of an experienced researcher would have made a crucial difference to progress.

Such stories from past educational research demonstrate that both theory and the applied professional practice have to start somewhere. The movers and shakers in the field of education could be any practitioner – or all! What makes the difference is the perspective of systematic reflection; an ethos of inquiry for improving all that practitioners understand, know and do. The ARC provides a framework which can prompt and support them to do this. The innovations of individuals provide the inspiration and the evidence base to impact on this professional standpoint, and ultimately to improve school experience and outcomes for students.

More recent stories of research

It may be helpful to revisit the very purpose of educational research from which to take a wider perspective of its place and its value to schools and other educational professionals. Both Bassey (1999) and, later, Rose (2011a) offer suggestions as to how research, through critical or systematic inquiry, informs educational theories, principles and practice leading to improved educational provision and learner outcomes. The scale of research and its findings can play out the whole spectrum of influence, great and small, for theory, policy and practice. The great educational theorists will all have built on the work of others, whatever the scale and perspective, but also, incrementally, taken their own steps of progress, once there was sufficient evidence to establish a sound basis from which to state claims and principles. The publications of such theorists show work spanning time as ideas emerge and are further developed and evidence substantiates or refutes research questions.

The direction and contribution of educational research continue to be discussed and contested (Hargreaves, 1996; Rose, 2011a, for example). Hargreaves claimed that most of this research 'does not make a serious contribution to fundamental theory or knowledge ... is irrelevant to practice' (1996, p. 7). He felt that educational research was distanced from practitioners, and that it was mainly reported in academic journals which few of them read. Rose (2011a, 2011b) responded to these suggestions by highlighting the huge importance of such research, *provided* it was clearly seated to respond to Hargreaves' claims. He described exemplars of research between schools and researchers, that: set out to contribute to the educational knowledge base; were completely relevant to and based in practice; built on previous research; were effectively disseminated by differing means to a range of audiences (e.g. social stories with learners with ASD; Howley, 2001; Howley and Arnold, 2005); and involved research exploring and documenting collaborative working in classrooms to promote greater inclusion (Doveston and Keenaghan, 2006a, 2006b).

Collaborative research between practitioners and academic researchers can bridge 'reality' gaps by focusing work *in situ* and involving frontline school staff and or students, for example. Rose (2011a, 2011b) explored this view of educational research that effects real change in schools, describing methods that enhance and promote the potential influences of this by including practitioners as part of the research team. Fergusson et al. (2004, 2006) and Rose et al. (2007), in very different studies, each highlight the valuable insights from teachers included in the research processes – whether as research partners, involved in piloting or carrying out trials of new materials, or contributing as key members of focus or reference groups. Work by Fergusson and her teacher associate partners explored the views and needs of teachers to be able to implement a national assessment strategy for learners with SEN. In response to findings, their work developed some well-trialled resources for training and support which were strongly influenced by a reference group of practitioners, who also undertook the drafting and piloting of these materials. The role of school partners in both of these studies ensured research was firmly placed within the reality of the school and responded to local and national educational contexts.

For practitioners and researchers, it is easy to believe that their own work may not have much impact beyond its own micro-context. They may not see that the knowledge, principles, theories and approaches they have routinely used in their regular practice will have started often from small beginnings. These small steps of professional development and learning accumulate to offer ideas that potentially provide the foundation of much bigger ideas, often at conceptual or theoretical levels. They may create the evidence to substantiate hypotheses and understandings, which eventually become established and common to practice and understandings.

In addition to the outcomes of such research and development, the invaluable lessons, and the new skills and opportunities, created through the actual process of research must not be overlooked. The very methodology, in its broadest sense, impacts on both personal and collective professional skills which, when applied elsewhere, can valuably influence school improvement towards more effective educational provision. However, such research activity needs careful planning and support. To be effective and to be meaningful, these research opportunities cannot happen successfully in a vacuum. Whether the research is very small-scale or of huge proportions, it is vital that the details are planned and shared in order to give it the best chances of success. The following case study explores some of these issues from a school context, examining practice fundamentals as to how research is viewed and valued across school communities and some of the more detailed practicalities.

Research in schools: a case study[1]

The Complex Learning Difficulties and Disabilities (CLDD) Research Project was a national research project undertaken by a core research team from the Schools Network in the UK and supported by the Department for Education (Carpenter et al., 2011). The research was carried out in partnership with 97 educational settings (including early years, special schools, and mainstream), in the UK and internationally. Its aim was to improve learning outcomes for students with the most complex educational needs and disabilities through the development of personalised learning pathways. The tools used for establishing these pathways were developed and trialled in collaboration with these schools based on the understanding of engagement as essential to learning (http://complexld.ssatrust.org.uk):

> Engagement is the single best predictor of successful learning for children with learning disabilities (Iovannone et al., 2003). Without engagement, there is no deep learning (Hargreaves, 2006), effective teaching, meaningful outcome, real attainment or quality progress (Carpenter, 2010). It is the essential platform for sustainable learning to occur.
>
> (Carpenter et al., 2011)

UK special schools were asked to apply to take part in the project, while smaller numbers of international special schools (the USA, Australia, New Zealand, Ireland, Scotland and Wales) and UK mainstream schools were approached directly. The number and quality of responses showed the interest and commitment many schools now have to school-based inquiry as a way of meeting the needs of an increasingly complex population of learners. With these learners, practitioners often need to adapt established approaches or innovate practice, and doing this systematically within a research framework allows them to create a strong, underpinning evidence base. The ARC was shared with the schools at the beginning of the project to bring the classical language of research, which is foreign to many practitioners, down to size – replacing it with related concepts associated with everyday practice in schools.

Michael Guralnick (2004), a professor at the University of Washington, recognises the role of the educator in the future of research. He refers to 'second generation' research that is 'practitioner led and evidence based'. He acknowledges the importance of practitioners' and young people's first-hand experiences in a daily setting, and the contribution this can make to increasing knowledge in the field and quality of practice.

At the end of the research project, the lead practitioner researchers in each school were invited to feed back on their own and their school's experiences of being involved in the research as part of a semi-structured exit interview. They answered a number of questions on what they and their students had taken from the research, and what advice they would offer to other schools becoming involved in such a project.

The importance of a supportive structure

The experiences of practitioners involved in the research suggested that one of the most critical elements for school-based research was a supportive structure (Carpenter, 2007). Those involved in the project felt the following contributed to success:

• The research carried out needed to be perceived as highly relevant to the setting (e.g. to students, practitioners, school policy) – if this were not the case, it was hard to justify the outlay in time.
• A high priority given to research by senior leadership – without the organisation prioritising rigorous research and its outcomes, teachers and teaching assistants struggled to balance conflicting demands.
• Staff needed to know their research was valued – regular research updates and project outcomes should be sought by senior leadership teams, and shared with parents and colleagues so that it had a whole-school and school community impact.
• The time and resource commitment needed to be recognised, acknowledged and supported at senior leadership level.
• The training implications needed acknowledging, both in undertaking research and in rolling out the outcomes of research more widely.

What practitioners gained from research

As a result of the research project, practitioners described how they had gained professionally.

Consistency of approach

One teacher described how, through the research, she had been able to address inconsistencies of approach among her teaching assistants. Each person in the class team felt that their approach was the right way of working with a particular student. Research allowed the teacher to show that, for that student, one way was more effective than the others. The classroom staff all wanted the best for that student, and so were willing to change their way of working once they could see the advantages of it. Thus practice was changed in an evidence-based, child-centred, non-confrontational way.

Continuing professional development

Practitioners reported that, for them, the process of research had been an in-depth professional development of great value. They suggested that class-based research should be incorporated into their school's rolling programme of continuing professional development (CPD), and given equal status with more traditional CPD.

Empowerment

One practitioner described how she had felt for some time that the school-wide approach to the teaching and learning of students with profound and multiple learning difficulties (PMLD) could be improved. Her research allowed her to focus upon specific areas of her students' learning and collect purposeful and systematic evidence to support an alternative approach. Based on this evidence, the head took her proposals to the school governors and effected a change in school policy. Without the research, the practitioner's opinion would have remained personal and unsubstantiated; her sharing outcomes brought great benefits to their learners with PMLD.

What schools gained from research

Practitioners thought that the research had led to the following outcomes:

- *School improvement* – Research enabled schools to bring an enhanced responsiveness to student need. It led to improved student learning and a solutions-focused approach from teaching staff. Systematic collection of evidence, and reflection on it, provided either an endorsement of current practice or indicated ways in which it could be changed.
- *Stronger professional teams* – Schools found that involvement in research increased communication and sharing of knowledge among class teams and with other colleagues, strengthening collaborative working and support. Two schools reported that, through being involved in research, their

teaching assistants had been able to increase the value of their observations about students.

- *Stronger evidence base for practice* – Through a rigorous evidence base, practitioners were able to justify their approaches to teaching in terms of the impact this had on students.

Advice on research from practitioners

Following their involvement in the research, practitioners were asked what advice they would give to colleagues about being involved in research. This resulted in the following list of key points:

- *Make sure you know what you are doing* – start the research as soon as you can (do not put it off!), and make sure you know what you are doing; if you leave everything to the last minute, the results will not be useful.
- *Do not go it alone* – if you have any difficulties or concerns, or do not understand anything, talk with colleagues. Ask questions until they are resolved.
- *Collect evidence regularly.*
- *Do not try to do it all yourself* – share your project with other teachers, teaching assistants and others who would like to be involved, otherwise it can be too burdensome.
- *Anything that is not written down is lost* – write down notes about your observations at the time. You may think you will remember it later but you will not!
- *Date everything!*

This advice came from experience. It ensures that the research is achievable, and that the hard work involved in gathering evidence is usable and not wasted.

Some of the advantages of this project for the schools taking part were that the checks for validity and rigour were carried out by the Schools Network core research team and an expert advisory team, and were not therefore the responsibility of the schools. These included: reading around what others had previously said about the research focus (engagement) and orientating this piece of research in relation to it; in association with the University of Northampton, drawing up an ethical code, and gaining approval for the project design (e.g. the research approach, collection and interpretation of research evidence, etc.); and sharing the outcomes of the project at the end. The school-based practitioner researchers within the project were involved in training days before and, in the earlier phases, additionally during the research period, where this information was shared and they had the opportunity to learn how to carry out the research and use the research tools.

Schools operating independently of a research team would need to take on these roles themselves underpinned by a research policy. For example, a school Research and Ethics Committee might include an academic representative from a local university and a practitioner from the school who has high level research experience, among others; someone within the school with research experience might be nominated as an adviser on research methods and procedure for other staff on research projects, supported by a local university link (Carpenter, 2007). The initial reading of relevant literature could be shared between a team of practitioners who were involved in research in the same area (Constable, personal communication, 2011), perhaps creating staff groups to read around and discuss the topic (McGill, 2010). With the current emphasis on school networking, there are more opportunities than ever for schools to share good practice at a number of levels (e.g. importantly with families, and among colleagues and governors, with other schools regionally, and nationally through presentations and papers). In this way, excellent practice does not remain in a few classrooms benefiting one or two learners, but can be a force for positive change for many practitioners and many students. Some regional authorities (e.g. North Yorkshire and Hertfordshire in the UK) are now working with schools in their area to establish multi-school research projects which promote an exciting research dynamic among their community of schools.

The way forward: opportunities for research

Practitioners may have the perception that there are very limited opportunities for research engagement within the classroom or school context. However, quite the opposite is so. In addition to opportunities created by the ongoing cycle of need to monitor and quality assure many aspects of school effectiveness at micro and macro levels, many practitioners are exploring research for the first time as part of their own professional development or post-qualification studies. These are often undertaken with universities or other higher education institutions, where a research component forms part of the learning and the accreditation requirement. Valuable experience and learning – about reviewing and critiquing literature and other documentation, on research design and methodology, for example – then become an additional set of flexible and useful tools for continued or varied application by that practitioner to improve and extend their practice or that of their school setting.

Such tools then enable practitioners and schools to make more systematic, research-oriented approaches to gather and analyse evidence or data, leading to more considered and informed decision-making in their routine practice. The very nature of framing research questions and hypotheses help to more clearly identify what it is practitioners really want or need to know. Exploring a range of observation methods and tools (e.g. time sampling the engagement levels of different student grouping as a means to identify the match between learners, activities and outcomes) creates real learning about research methods and analysis of data that will have a direct impact and lead to improved teaching and learning, but all within the everyday routine of the classroom context. By using a combination of research methods, schools may more effectively meet the needs of students and the wider community. Questionnaires, surveys, focus groups and interviews enable the meaningful gathering and analysis of views from diverse groups – staff, students and families, external and allied professionals and local neighbours, for example. This information provides a strong starting point from which to develop and evaluate any new initiatives. For example, Fergusson and Duffield (2001, 2003) successfully involved families in designing and delivering a curriculum to meet the diverse cultural and linguistic needs of students for whom English was not their home language. Their intentions and initiatives were validated by the views of their whole school community and the new programme was successful from the outset.

All of the stories from school-based research presented in this book have alluded to a positive ethos towards and valuing of research. This aspect of the research context can be a strong influence on the plausibility and potential success of any research undertaking. There has been advice from practitioner researchers – that it was imperative to have the involvement and support of the school's senior leaders/managers; to enable the practitioner to have the flexibility and time to address the practical elements of their investigations; to be open and responsive to the research findings; to establish the training and support necessary for the professionals involved to carry out the research tasks appropriately; to offer opportunities for the research to be disseminated among the school community and ultimately, to have an impact on educational provision and outcomes. Hargreaves (2001) adds a note of reality, reiterating that each stage of the research process takes time, plus he cautions that it will not be successful if practitioners feel overworked and neglected, nor if their efforts are unrewarded!

Collaborative research networks

Professional bodies and networks (e.g. subject associations or organisations relating to specific student populations, by phase or disability perhaps), in addition to offering their specialist support through various forums, more frequently highlight common issues, challenges and initiatives. These present potential research opportunities that could be explored collaboratively by or with their own communities. The communities themselves, in this age of technology, present international dimensions and opportunities – to both learn from and engage with research itself through internet collaboration.

Many such organisations and networks actively facilitate research as a means of furthering their specialist focus; some even have designated special interest research groups. Indeed, one such network, the PMLD Network, currently operates via an internet forum (http://www.pmldnetwork.org/). It focuses on supporting and improving the lives of people with profound and multiple learning disabilities, including educational provision. It has been a forum for sharing ideas and issues in practice for about five years, when it first originated. More and more, forum members have been posting queries and offering challenges in an effort to improve practice, knowledge and understanding in this very narrow field of education, where so often everyone working in this area feels isolated. Very recently an off-shoot development has been the creation of a sub-group for those interested in collaborating in research in this field. It offered an open invitation to practitioners, new and experienced researchers, family carers and other interested parties to share the common aim to 'move things forward' for the better. Within days of the group being created, there was suddenly easy access to training and to relevant literature and information about international research in this field; members offering support or to share research resources; and with outcomes being disseminated straight to the field immediately research is completed. Already it has established a reciprocal exchange, for what Hargreaves (2001) describes as 'mutual growth'.

Potential for research collaboration lies not only with our professional peers, but under our noses! Practitioners can learn much from involving their own students – either by researching their views and responses or, more excitingly, by working with them in research partnerships. Byers et al. (2008) describe innovative participative action research, where children and young people with learning disabilities worked as co-researchers with the project research team in nine inclusive secondary schools and colleges across England. The research followed a person-centred approach (O'Brien and Lyle O'Brien, 1988), with the student firmly at the heart of the research. The 'research team' of teachers and students in each educational context set their own agenda, using an accessible version of the Action Research Cycle (see Figure 11.1). As the ARC seeks to do for practitioners, the language used in the Accessible Action Research Cycle removed the barriers to inclusion of young people as researchers by replacing the classical research language with similar everyday concepts that related to their experience.

The young people's own opinions and insights of how their experience at school or college could be improved informed the research planning and design. School staff acted as facilitators throughout the research, rather than in their more usual roles of direct teaching or leading the learning process. Both staff and student researchers were supported by the project research team at each

Figure 11.1 The Accessible Action Research Cycle
Source: Byers et al. (2008).

stage of the action research, and then in reporting their outcomes through several collaborative dissemination events. The development of the project website was also the result of collaboration by all partners, using research methods in consultation. Each of the nine settings demonstrated change instigated by the student researchers, facilitated by the teacher researchers. Many of these schools and colleges continue to draw on the research approaches in their everyday practice because they saw dramatic improvements in student engagement and their learning experience.

The influences of this research may lead to wider outcomes with students and teachers disseminating this work to policy-makers in their local regions and on a national stage, supported by a targeted policy briefing paper (Morgan and Byers, 2008). The direct involvement of teachers and students in this research created a sense of joint ownership of the project. Their research activity as part of a partnership offered roles with responsibility and accountability. In turn, these created opportunities that empowered both students and teachers. The research enabled them to keep an open mind when examining their situations and to look for constructive solutions by reframing the issues with research questions. The research led to their thinking and their views and expectations being challenged. School staff and students alike were very motivated because the research was so meaningful and so important to them all. Their research met with great success and really made a positive difference.

The value of support

Finding the right support for researchers will give any project the best chances of success. Support from 'more experienced' colleagues or a research mentor is likely to keep any project more focused and realistic, and its outcomes more reliable and relevant. Many practitioner researchers establish research relationships with academic researchers/tutors, which continue beyond their formal studies. Many universities, other institutions and research communities offer support networks that welcome practitioner colleagues. Such networks and partnerships have often been created as a result of collaborative projects between schools and university researchers, where schools over time and with experience, develop a real research ethos and culture. Roles within such partnerships demonstrate reciprocal learning and sharing, with roles seen as equal but complementary – each has a valuable part to play in the researching process in the school (Fergusson and Cullingford-Agnew, 2005).

The role of action research as a form of continuing professional development is discussed by Cordingley et al. (2003). However, to be most effective, they advocate that practitioner researchers would benefit most not from a trainer, but rather a supporter. They suggest a 'facilitative model' would be most useful where there is a clear sharing of ideas, yet the supporter offers a challenge to current thinking and practice in order to seek solutions. They continue with the premise that action research begins *in* practice; the evidence base developed is about practising what we preach as theories from the research arise out of the practice itself. It acts as a vehicle to investigate and challenge what is currently done. With the development of more case studies on practice, a more powerful basis for knowledge will accrue, with potentially profound possibilities for the future. Not only can personally focused or small-scale changes occur, but broader, organisational and systemic change may be a direct consequence of action research.

McNiff (2002) suggests seeking critical friends or validation groups through which practitioners can get informed feedback about their research. She discusses their value in helping to evaluate the quality of research, offering critical and constructive feedback or making professional judgements about the validity of research findings and as importantly, interpretations of these. She talks of 'the power of sharing ideas to generate new ones' and likens research to a 'conduit for learning' (2002, p. 15), with ideas and learning being influenced by others when working together. The strongest research has a focus not solely on the actions and outcomes, but importantly also on the learning process involved. It is implied that the process of questioning is of equal importance to the generation of answers. The role played by practitioner-researchers adds to this value, because they are taking the responsibility for researching their own practice; responding to their own questions, as the practitioners have done in the preceding chapters.

Meaningful dissemination

Many of the stories of research cited across the book are of 'everyday' small-scale practitioner research and many of them will go unnoticed, because they are not disseminated effectively. There will be many more that may stray into descriptive and anecdotal reportings – these are even less likely to have any impact. Yet, if they were to be shared with professional and educational communities, evidence-based practice could begin to be more substantiated.

Rose (2011a, 2011b) and Hargreaves (2001) offer strategies to ensure dissemination is most productive in both reaching its target group and in its impact. Rose highlighted the importance of demonstrating the relevance of research to education practitioners and the need to match the reporting style to each target audience. Hargreaves adds another angle, by suggesting 'champions' who are viewed as professionally credible to undertake the dissemination, where possible by demonstrating and not simply explaining the research findings. To address these fundamental issues and bring about the most effective dissemination, would-be researchers need to give real consideration to this and build a clear planned response into their action research cycle as suggested by the ARC. This may take the form of a range of dissemination activities to meet the diverse needs and expectations of different parts of the professional field and communities. To demonstrate a very wide range of large- and small-scale dissemination, take the example of Byers and colleagues in their 'What about us?' project (2008), where the activities were tailored to the strengths of the wider research team and to fit the specific needs of their audiences. They undertook a number of dissemination events with the young student co-researchers and their school staff – to their own school and college communities, nationally with each other and also on a national stage, to policy-makers and key educationalists. Published outputs from this research again met differing needs; the student researchers reported their work in school and college newsletters and magazines, the school staff shared their perspectives with their mainstream peers through local/regional networks and clusters and local education authority bulletins: they were routinely featured in local press and TV media news. The academic researchers with school staff contributed to a final report (Byers et al., 2008), a policy briefing paper (Morgan and Byers, 2008) and a peer-reviewed publication in an academic journal (Lewis et al., 2008). The whole project team collaboratively developed the project website www.whataboutus.org.uk, each taking a role matched to their interests and strengths – some choosing the photos, finding out about people's preferences for font, text sizes, colour and lay-out; others writing and reporting the project findings.

Schools and practitioners who are 'active researchers' are in a strong position to have influence within their own professional context. Where there is a sound evidence base and effective dissemination, this influence may be far-reaching – to other, or all, schools and policy-makers. The further development and embedding of research engagement into teaching practices and school-based review may reinstate the professional position and expertise of practitioners as clear agents of change.

The notion of educational research coalitions as the way forward is illustrated by Haslam (2010). He describes the work of the Institute for Effective Education, which encourages practitioners, academic researchers and policy-makers to work together across the whole education community. There will certainly continue to be a need for school-based action research and if practitioners have the strength of an infrastructures such as this, then they will have a supported and valued role – from the start.

The cycle of action research, by its very nature, is self-perpetuating. An audit of practice will reveal what is missing and generate the need to develop something new, that new idea needs to be trialled and implemented, which in turn then needs to be evaluated ... and suddenly the start of that cycle comes round again. Or, maybe it's not so much a circular cycle but rather a spiral of research because practitioners are progressing onto new territory with each next step.

Action research, like other research approaches, can be mapped within the ARC. The stages of the ARC, with its accessible language, reminds practitioners of all the elements of classical research which need attention if school-based research is to be robust, but is expressed in a way which resonates with their own experiences. Many of the activities that practitioners carry out every day through planning, assessing and recording, and so on, are the blocks with which they can build systematic exploration and inquiry. To meet the needs of the most challenged learners, practitioners will increasingly need to explore new and enhanced approaches to deliver their educational entitlement and be able to trial, adapt and evidence their effectiveness using systematic inquiry.

So with that in mind, let us return to one of the original stories of research from the past and consider the practice of Intensive Interaction (Hewett, 1986) which, through research, developed to promote positive communicative interactions with students who have learning disabilities. As stated above, within the field, this approach is now established and considered common practice, with many practitioners publishing literature about how to use it. Yet thirty years on there is little evaluative evidence of the approach to systematically and objectively gauge its real benefits ... sounds like this is the challenge of the next piece of practitioner-led inquiry!

Note

1   This section was contributed by Jo Egerton, The Schools Network, London.

References

Barber, M. (2011) Making interactions: Intensive Interaction. *Intensive Interaction Down Under Newsletter*, 7(4), 1–7.

Bassey, M. (1999) *Case Study Research in Educational Settings*. Buckingham: Open University Press.

Byers, R., Davies, J., Fergusson, A. and Marvin, C. (2008) *What About Us? Promoting Emotional Well-Being and Inclusion by Working with Young People with Learning Difficulties in Schools and Colleges*. London: Foundation for People with Learning Disabilities/University of Cambridge. Available at: www.whataboutus.org.uk.

Carpenter, B. (2007) Developing the role of schools as research organisations: the Sunfield experience. *British Journal of Special Education*, 34, 67–76.

Carpenter, B. (2010) *A vision for the 21st Century Special School*. London: Specialist Schools and Academies Trust (now The Schools Network).

Carpenter, B., Egerton, J., Brooks, T., Cockbill, B., Fotheringham, J., & Rawson, H. (2011) *The Complex Learning Difficulties and Disabilities Research Project: Developing Pathways to Personalised Learning*. London: Specialist Schools and Academies Trust (now The Schools Network). [Online at: http:complexld.ssatrust.org.uk; accessed: 24.11.11.]

Cordingley, P., Bell, M., Rundell, B. and Evans, D. (2003) The impact of collaborative CPD on classroom teaching and learning. In *Research Evidence in Education Library*. London: EPPI-Centre, Social Science Research Unit, Institute of Education, University of London.

Doveston, M. and Keenaghan, M. (2006a) Improving classroom dynamics to support students' learning and social inclusion: a collaborative approach. *Support for Learning*, 21(1), 5–11.

Doveston, M. and Keenaghan, M. (2006b) Growing Talent for Inclusion: using an appreciative inquiry approach into investigating classroom dynamics. *Journal of Research in Special Educational Needs*, 6(3), 153–165.

Fergusson, A. and Cullingford-Agnew, S. (2005) Developing practice through reflection: a model for training. Paper presented at ECER, Dublin, Ireland, 6–10 Sept.

Fergusson, A. and Duffield, T. (2001) Promoting cultural, religious and linguistic diversity in a special school. In R. Rose and I. Grosvenor (eds) *Doing Research in Special Education*. London: David Fulton.

Fergusson, A. and Duffield, T. (2003) Including cultural and linguistic diversity in a specialist school for pupils with severe learning difficulties. In T. Tilstone and R. Rose (eds) *Strategies to Promote Inclusive Practice*. London: Routledge.

Fergusson, A., Green, J. and Leeson, S. (2004) Collaborative working to promote inclusive practice. Paper presented to The European Dimension of Special Education conference, Thessaloniki, Greece, 18–23 Nov.

Fergusson, A., Green, J. and Leeson, S. (2006) *Supporting the Use of the P Scales in the East Midlands Region: Final Report*. Northampton: University of Northampton.

Foreman-Peck, L. (2005) Do teachers need research? In R. Barrow and L. Foreman-Peck (eds) *What Use Is Educational Research?* London: Philosophy of Education Society of Great Britain.

Guralnick, M. (2004) Early intervention for children with disabilities. Keynote address to the 12th IASSID World Congress, Montpellier, France, June.

Hargreaves, D. (1996) Teaching as a research based profession: possibilities and prospects. TTA Annual Lecture, London.

Hargreaves, D. (2001) The knowledge creating school. In B. Moon, J. Butcher, and E. Bird (eds) *Leading Professional Development in Education*. London: Routledge Falmer.

Hargreaves, D. (2006) *A new Shape for Schooling?* London: Specialist Schools and Academies Trust (now The Schools Network).

Haslam, J. (2010) Bringing evidence into the classroom. *Better Evidence-based Education. Social-Emotional Learning*. Winter, 22–23.

Hewett, D. (1986) *Understanding Experience*. Newsletter No. 5. Cambridge: Cambridge Institute of Education.

Hewett, D. and Nind, M. (1988) Developing an interactive curriculum for pupils with severe and complex learning difficulties. In B. Smith (ed.) *Interactive Approaches to the Education of Children with Severe Learning Difficulties*. Birmingham: Westhill College.

Hewett, D. and Nind, M. (1989) Interaction as curriculum at Harperbury School. *PMLD Link 5*.

Howley, M. (2001) An investigation into the impact of social stories on the behaviour and social understanding of four pupils with autistic spectrum disorder. In R. Rose and I. Grosvenor (eds) *Doing Research in Special Education*. London: David Fulton.

Howley, M. and Arnold, E. (2005) *Revealing the Hidden Social Code*. London: Jessica Kingsley.

Iovannone, R., Dunlap, G., Huber, H., and Kincaid, D. (2003) Effective educational practices for students with autism specturm disorder. *Focus on Autism and other Developmental Disabilities*, 18, 150–166.

Jones, K.R. (1972) Rebus materials in pre-school playgroups. *Teachers' Research Groups Journal*. Bristol: Research Unit, School of Education, University of Bristol.

Lewis, A., Parsons, S., Robertson, C., Feiler, A., Tarleton, B., Watson, D., et al. (2008) Reference, or advisory, groups involving disabled people: reflections from three contrasting research projects. *British Journal of Special Education*, 35(2), 78–84.

Lindsley, O.R. (1968) Training parents and teachers to precisely manage children's behavior. In *Special Education Colloquium*. Flint, MI: C.S. Mott Foundation, pp. 42–53.

Longhorn, F. (1988) *A Sensory Curriculum for Very Special People*. London: Souvenir Press.

McBrien, J. and Weightman, J. (1980) The effect of room management procedures on the engagement of profoundly retarded children. *British Journal of Mental Subnormality*, 26(50, Pt 1), 38–46.

McGill, P. (2010) Case study: a shared vision. In B. Carpenter, *A Vision for 21st Century Special Education (Complex Needs Series No. 1)*. London: Specialist Schools and Academies Trust (now The Schools Network).

McNiff , J. (2002) *Action Research for Professional Development: Concise Advice for New Action Researchers*, 3rd edn. Available at: http://www.jeanmcniff.com/ar-booklet.asp (accessed 13.3.2011).

Morgan, H. and Byers, R. (2008) *What about Us? Promoting Emotional Well-Being and Inclusion by Working with Young People with Learning Difficulties in Schools and Colleges*. Summary Briefing: Need 2 Know Series. London: Foundation for People with Learning Disabilities/University of Cambridge.

Nind, M. and Hewett, D. (1988) Interaction as curriculum. *British Journal of Special Education*, 15(2), 55–57.

O'Brien, J. and Lyle O'Brien, C. (1988) *A Little Book about Person Centred Planning*. Toronto: Inclusion Press.

Rose, R. (2011a) Establishing the relationship between research and practice in education. Presentation to Annual School of Education PhD Student Conference, University of Northampton, UK, May.

Rose, R. (2011b) Research that affects change, Special Educational Needs. Presentation to Research with Impact; Researcher Learning at Work Day, University of Northampton, UK, June.

Rose, R., Howley, M., Fergusson, A. and Jament, J. (2007) *Making Sense of Mental Health: The Emotional Wellbeing of Children and Young People with Complex Needs in Schools*. NASS Research Final Report. Northampton: University of Northampton.

Ullmann, L.P. and Krasner, L. (eds) (1965) *Case Studies in Behavior Modification*. New York: Holt, Rinehart & Winston.

van Oosterom, J. and Devereux, K. (1982) REBUS at Rees Thomas School. *Special Education: Forward Trends*, 9(1), 31–33.

Index

The **bold** page numbers denote Figures or Tables.